# The American Literacy Profile Scales

## A Framework for Authentic Assessment

**Patrick Griffin**
**Patricia G. Smith**
**Lois E. Burrill**

Heinemann

Heinemann
A division of Reed Elsevier Inc.
361 Hanover Street
Portsmouth, NH 03801-3912

*Offices and agents throughout the world*

Published simultaneously in 1995
in the United States of America by Heinemann
and in Australia by
Robert Andersen & Associates Pty Ltd
433 Wellington Street
Clifton Hill
Victoria 3068

CIP is on file with the Library of Congress
ISBN: 0-435-08831-9

Designed by Colin Wilson
Illustrations by Colin Wilson and Margaret Nicoll
Cover design by Sharon Carr, Graphic Divine, Elwood, Victoria,
Australia
Typeset in 12/14pt Bembo by Publishing Innovations, Springhill,
Victoria, Australia
Printed in Hong Kong by Colorcraft Ltd

# Contents

● ● ● ● ● ● ● ● ● ● ● ● ● ● ● ● ● ● ● ● ● ● ● ● ● ● ● ● ● ● ● ● ● ● ● ● ● ● ● ● ● ● ● ● ● ● ● ● ● ● ● ● ● ● ● ● ● ● ●

# Preface

The literacy profiles were begun in Victoria, Australia, in 1986, when the research section of the Victorian Ministry of Education began a search for a system of monitoring achievement in schools. After almost five years of research and development, the first *Victorian Literacy Profiles Handbook* appeared; then followed several years of successful monitoring of school achievements. It became clear that profiling as a system of monitoring in schools also had a positive effect on teaching and learning.

Several further projects were launched, including numeracy profiles and national profiles. The Australian government adopted the idea comprehensively and developed compulsory assessment through profiles for all schools.

The profiles are descriptive, not prescriptive. The norms illustrate what is normal development for average students. No attempt is made to impose standards. Despite the benefit of such benchmarks, years of monitoring with standardized tests have not had an impact on standards to any great extent, so teachers now are given the opportunity to define what is desirable at individual student levels. Optimum and even maximum rates of progress can be attained and monitored, regardless of standards.

At international conferences and at workshops with teachers in the United States, Canada, the United Kingdom, Ireland, Vietnam, Hong Kong, China and Scandinavia, the idea of profiling has steadily developed and taken hold. After several workshops and surveys in the United States, it was decided to develop a set of profiles that would serve the needs of American schools. Dr Lois Burrill has been associated with the authors of the profiles since long before the idea even began; she has worked with Patrick Griffin in literacy and assessment since 1980, and these fifteen years have seen many ideas develop — none more powerful than the idea of profiles that combine all the recent developments in measurement and assessment, and in curriculum monitoring.

After two years of work in the United States gathering teacher input and data on student development with the profiles, it has been possible to make the appropriate adjustments and to provide guiding data for American teachers. Further work to develop the scales, such as in viewing and listening, will be needed: these are projects the authors have set themselves for the future in the United States. Meanwhile, teachers will continue to make known what is needed in the profiles and in establishing appropriate uses for the scales.

We hope that this series of scales will have a positive effect on teaching and learning, and that the distinction between teaching and assessment will disappear — to the benefit of both teachers and students.

# Acknowledgments

A book such as this cannot emerge without the help of literally thousands of people. Teachers, students, researchers, publishers and editors have all contributed to the exercise.

The Ministry of Education in Victoria, Australia, graciously agreed to the use of some of the original scales. They have been modified a little, but their success made it next to impossible to produce anything different — so the format remains, as does much of the content. Over the years that the scales have been in use we have received good feedback; most focused on the use of contextual information, the gap between bands D and E and the possibility of developing scales for second-language learning.

Workshops with teachers and with administrators have all contributed to the improvement of the profiles, but the most benefit has been received from users — the teachers who have shown us real applications in the classroom and how they report to parents, to administrators and to governments. These applications have been incorporated into the book.

Unlike the first handbook, this manual is based on practise. The first books were based on the authors' intuition and experience; by and large they were correct, but there can be no better advice than that which is considered good practise by users of the scales, and these people must be thanked.

Unfortunately, the great number of teachers from several countries who lent their experience and wisdom to the project makes it impossible to identify individually all who have contributed. There are, however, many who did special work for the project, particularly when time was pressing towards publication date. Jean Shultz worked hard developing ideas and trying them out in special education classes. Anne Hammond developed a range of exercises and advice for reading classes, and Bryan O'Reilly identified the breakthrough approaches to the teaching of writing associated with the profiles. John Byrne helped the teachers in northern New York to develop databases, as did Mary Driver, Joanne Scharre, Paula Fleming, Anne McCallum, Mary Vietch and Audrey Farnsworth. Without these people, it would not be possible to give teachers the advice they need in using profiles in the classroom.

Other teachers whose help is acknowledged with gratitude are as follows:

Carmel Allen, Yvonne Allen, Mary Ange, Jan Arnott, Carolyn Bartlow, Dennis Bastian, Peggy Boschma, Val Brittain, Phil Bryan, Reta S. Burns, John Burns, Nancy Campbell, Margaret Connell, Carol Coon, Marcia Cottrell, Sandra Croft, Carol Davie, Marijean Eye, Ross Grant, Kerry Hazell, Joan Hitt, Cathy Hood, Catherine Johnson, Pat Jordan, Hilary Kent, Beverly Kirpatrick, Priscilla Lawrence, Pauline Lee, Margrita Maier, Ros McArthur, Kathy McLean, James Miller, Jan Miller, Joan Mills, Lisa Moore, Helen Nissner, Peter Nix, Sue O'Brien, David Palumbo, Mary Ann Paton, Christine Powers, Cynthia Ritlinger, David Rule, Connie Russell, Monica Rylance, Sarah Salter, Anne Smyth, Cheryl Southwick, Linda Stephens, Heather Stewart, Marie Stobaugh, Jo Sullivan, Michael Sullivan, Michelle Susat, Paul Thompson, Marie Tills, Phil Toner, Tina Torcello, Marg Treloar, Veronica Tuncay, Ann Watts, Esther Wiggins, Karen Wilson, Bonnie Witt, Fay Woods, Marg Wright.

**SECTION 1**

# Profiles and assessment

# CHAPTER 1
# What is a profile?

In simple terms, a profile is a scale depicting progress in learning. There are five profile scales of literacy, to cover reading, writing, spoken language, listening and viewing; each scale covers nine levels — labelled from A (lowest) to I (highest) — and presents, at each level and in each area, a nutshell (summary) statement and a detailed description, called a *band*.

Profiles are designed to assist teachers, schools and systems with the complex process of assessment, recording and reporting of students' developing competencies and achievements.

An essential feature of a student's profile is that it shows growth. Through its ordered sequence of bands, it makes explicit what progress in learning means. It provides a framework against which evidence of progress of an individual can be charted and achievements of a school — or even an education system — can be monitored.

Figure 1.1 highlights the overall structure of a profile scale using the nutshell statements for writing as an example. Details of the component parts — bands, nutshells and contexts — are presented in later sections that contain the classroom guidelines and materials and show the nutshell statements linked to bands of development. The nutshell encourages teachers to work first from an overview or holistic approach, focusing on levelness, and then to use the detailed bands as an indicative list of behaviors that signal growth. In short, we work from the nutshell to the detail, and then try to build the profile.

A complete set of nutshell statements and detailed bands is included in appendixes I and II.

| | Bands | Nutshell statements |
|---|---|---|
| **Dimension of achievement and developing competence** | **I** •••••••• | Writes in many genres. Masters the craft of writing. Is capable of powerful writing. |
| | **H** •••••••• | Is aware of subtleties in language. Develops analytical arguments. Uses precise descriptions in writing. Edits to sharpen meaning. |
| | **G** •••••••• | Uses rich vocabulary, writing style depends on topic, purpose and audience. Writing is lively and colorful. Can do major revisions of writing. |
| | **F** •••••••• | Can describe things well. Can skillfully write and tell a story or describe phenomena. Now has skills to improve writing. |
| | **E** •••••••• | Can plan, organize and polish writing. Writes in paragraphs. Vocabulary and grammar are suited to topic. Can write convincing stories. |
| | **D** •••••••• | Can write own stories. Changes words and spelling until satisfied with result. |
| | **C** •••••••• | Now says something in own writing. Is writing own sentences. Is taking interest in appearance of writing. |
| | **B** •••••••• | Is learning about handwriting. Knows what letters and words are and can talk about ideas in own writing. Is starting to write recognizable letters and words. |
| | **A** •••••••• | Knows that writing says something. Is curious about environmental print. Is starting to see patterns. |

*Figure 1.1*

The relationship between the nutshell and the band is shown in the following illustration of one level (E) in each of the reading and writing bands; an example of how the profiles are presented for teachers' use is given on page 5.

# Reading band E

## Nutshell

**Will tackle difficult texts. Writing and general knowledge reflect reading. Literary response reflects confidence in settings and characters.**

• • • • • • • • • • • • • • • • • • • • • • • • • • •

## Band

### Reading strategies

Reads to others with few inappropriate pauses. Interprets new words by reference to suffixes, prefixes and meaning of word parts. Uses directories such as a table of contents or an index, or telephone and street directories, to locate information. Uses library classification systems to find specific reading materials.

### Responses

Improvises in role play, drawing on a range of text. Writing shows meaning inferred from the text. Explains a piece of literature. Expresses and supports an opinion on whether an author's point of view is valid. Discusses implied motives of characters in the text. Makes comments and expresses feelings about characters. Rewrites information from text in own words. Uses text as a model for own writing. Uses a range of books and print materials as information sources for written work. Reads aloud with expression.

• • • • • • • • • • • • • • • • • • • • • • • • • • •

# Writing band E

## Nutshell

**Can plan, organize and polish writing. Writes in paragraphs. Vocabulary and grammar are suited to the topic. Can write convincing stories.**

• • • • • • • • • • • • • • • • • • • • • • • • • • •

## Band

### What the writer does

Edits work to a point where others can read it; corrects common spelling errors, punctuation and grammatical errors. Develops ideas into paragraphs. Uses a dictionary, thesaurus or word-checker to extend and check vocabulary for writing. Uses vivid, specific language.

### What the writing shows

Sentences with ideas that flow. Paragraphs with a cohesive structure. Ability to present relationships and to argue or persuade. Messages in expository and argumentative writing identifiable by others, although some information may be omitted. Brief passages written with clear meaning, accuracy of spelling and apt punctuation. Appropriate shifts from first to third person in writing. Consistent use of the correct tense. Appropriate vocabulary for familiar audiences such as peers, younger children or adults, with only occasional inappropriate word choice. Compound sentences, using conjunctions. Variations of letters, print styles or fonts. A print style appropriate to task and a consistent handwriting style.

### Use of writing

Writes a properly sequenced text that has a convincing setting. Creates characters from imagination.

• • • • • • • • • • • • • • • • • • • • • • • • • • •

In chapters 4 to 8, the bands are collected in pages that present three levels. This has been done because in our experience with the profiles it is common for a class to be spread over three or four bands and for any individual student to exhibit behaviours described by indicators from within several adjacent bands. Hence, the profile record sheet becomes a recording procedure for teachers. The sheets are presented as blackline masters and teachers are encouraged to copy them, mark them with a highlighter pen and store them in students' portfolios.

Of the five profile scales presented, those for reading and writing have been in use for some years; the spoken language scale is new, but has had considerable use. Performance data has been collected for these scales and is presented in graphic form in Chapter 10. The listening and viewing scales have been prepared specifically for this book and as yet have had little use. They are in essence experimental. Figure 1.2 encapsulates the history and experience of the series of profile scales.

Following chapters 1 and 2, the second section of the book first describes how to use the profiles and then presents the profile scales together with suggested authentic assessment contexts to use in the classroom. The format of chapters 4 to 6 consists of two-page units; on the left-hand page, teachers are presented with the nutshell and the contexts and on the right-hand page are the bands of the profile scales.

Chapters 7 and 8 presents the nutshells and bands for viewing and listening.

The third section presents information on recording and reporting to a range of audiences,

COMMENT

# Writing band D

### What the writer does
Marks most common words with incorrect spelling when editing writing. Uses ideas, themes and structure from books in writing. Uses concepts of order and time in writing. Reads, rereads and revises own written work. Uses everyday words in appropriate written context.

### What the writing shows
Punctuation used conventionally. Conventional spelling used most of the time; spelling showing recall of visual patterns. Stories that can be read, understood and retold by classmates. Several sentences constructed on one topic in a logical order. A smooth connection of ideas. Beginning, middle and end in narrative writing.

### Use of writing
Writes stories containing characters from outside personal environment. Writes with ease on most matters of personal experience. Writes on a variety of topics. Writes personal anecdotes and letters to friends. Writes for a known audience. Uses a range of written forms — poems, letters, journals, logs, etc.

COMMENT

# Writing band E

### What the writer does
Edits work to a point where others can read it; corrects common spelling errors, punctuation and grammatical errors. Develops ideas into paragraphs. Uses a dictionary, thesaurus or word-checker to extend and check vocabulary for writing. Uses vivid, specific language.

### What the writing shows
Sentences with ideas that flow. Paragraphs with a cohesive structure. Ability to present relationships and to argue or persuade. Messages in expository and argumentative writing identifiable by others, although some information may be omitted. Brief passages written with clear meaning, accuracy of spelling and apt punctuation. Appropriate shifts from first to third person in writing. Consistent use of the correct tense. Appropriate vocabulary for familiar audiences such as peers, younger children or adults, with only occasional inappropriate word choice. Compound sentences, using conjunctions. Variations of letters, print styles or fonts. A print style appropriate to task and a consistent handwriting style.

### Use of writing
Writes a properly sequenced text that has a convincing setting. Creates characters from imagination.

COMMENT

# Writing band F

### What the writer does
Writes sentences in different forms: statement, question, command, explanation. Writes paragraphs to develop logical sequence of ideas. Corrects most spelling, punctuation and grammatical errors in editing others' written work. Consults available sources to improve or enhance writing. Joins letters, using linkages where appropriate, to form personal handwriting style.

### What the writing shows
Narratives containing introduction, complication and resolution in a logical order. Longer descriptions and narratives developed coherently. Use of both active and passive voice. A range of vocabulary and grammatical structures. Complex sentences — principal and subordinate clauses. Higher level writing skills in areas of special interest. Understanding of the difference between narrative and other forms of writing.

### Use of writing
Completes standard forms requiring personal information. Makes appropriate use of narrative and other forms of writing.

# Suggested new indicators

VIEWING · LISTENING · SPOKEN LANGUAGE · WRITING · READING

A B C D E F G H I

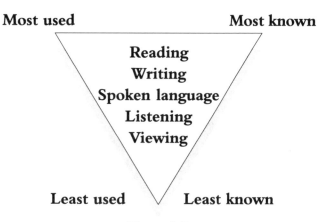

Most used          Most known

Reading
Writing
Spoken language
Listening
Viewing

Least used       Least known

*Figure 1.2*

shows how the scales might be used for children with special needs and discusses the reading classroom and normative data on teacher judgment.

Following appendixes I and II, a further set of blackline masters is presented to enable teachers and administrators to make records and to adapt for reporting purposes.

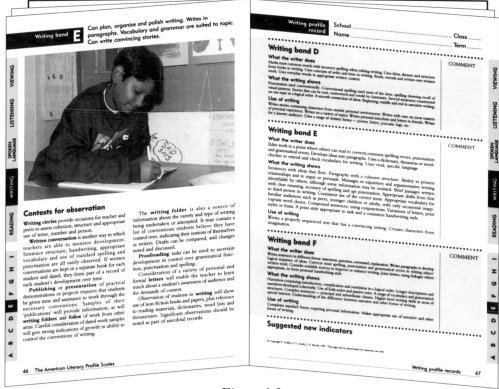

*Figure 1.3*

# Properties of profiles

1 Profiles are holistic. Because they incorporate many kinds of learning, they allow communication of the widest span of learning outcomes, viz., the cognitive, affective, aesthetic and practical.

2 The focus of profiles is to demonstrate competence, regardless of how it has been acquired, rather than to detail course content or be instruments of measurement. This can be across subjects and contexts, in school or at home. It does not relate to the nature of the curriculum or to the content of the texts, reading materials or the process being taught. Experience with the literacy profiles in three countries with widely varying curricula attest to their robustness in this regard.

3 The distinctive feature of profiles is that what is to be achieved is described explicitly. For example, in the scales for writing and reading an extensive range of achievement from early stages to mastery is shown regardless of how that achievement has been assessed or learnt, or of the curriculum in which the learning took place.

4 They include higher order outcomes of knowledge and skills. There is an attempt to go beyond the variations of the curriculum delivered in classrooms and to describe those things that are important for all students to know and be able to do, regardless of the details of the program that they pursue.

5 Profiles allow for a wide range of both formal methods of student assessment (tests and related assessment tasks) and informal methods (observations and descriptive judgments), typically used by teachers, to be calibrated and mapped onto a common developmental scale. Using recent developments in item response theory (IRT) the major advantage of the scales is that they enable students' performances on different tasks to be compared reliably — from student to student and from year to year.

6 Profiles provide a framework for the interpretation and communication of the huge amount of assessment information available to teachers — a way of synthesizing teachers' judgments of a wide array of formal and informal assessments. They are particularly useful for interpreting performance assessment and portfolios.

7 Profiles can serve both formative and summative functions. The process of compiling profile data can be of formative use in that it may help the teaching and learning process; the product can serve summative requirements by providing overall indices of achievement for a student or group of students.

8 Profiles are often treated as qualitative, but can have quantitative components. Where there are quantitative components, data may be aggregated across subjects and/or students.

9 The interpretation of profiles is primarily criterion-referenced, but norm-referenced interpretation is sometimes also possible. Moderation, or teacher comparison of evidence and justification of judgments, is central to the application of profiling. This in turn has implications for both formal and informal professional development of teachers.

10 Finally, profiles may be motivating for students, since motivation is enhanced by emphasis on positive achievements and by allocating to the student some degree of responsibility for the compilation of the profile. Teachers may be similarly motivated by the validation profiles give their judgment and by their usefulness in identifying the positive aspects of student learning.

# CHAPTER 2
# Development and uses of profiles: an overview

The process of profiling the literacy growth of individual students has its greatest rewards for individual teachers and groups of teachers in an individual building, although the resulting profiles may also be aggregated to provide information about the larger school district, region and so on. Throughout this manual many uses of profiles will be mentioned, for both formative and summative assessment purposes. Some of those purposes are briefly mentioned here.

When classroom teachers are planning their next lessons and units, their knowledge of each student, based on the profiles, may enable them to target particular activities or lessons for particular students, and to group students for short periods to work on particular goals highlighted by the profile achievement patterns. The understandings gleaned from the profiles may help them to adjust time schedules to meet the needs of the current year's group.

The profiles may be particularly useful to the classroom teacher as he or she begins to complete report cards for the class and to write individual comments for each of the students. In the same way, the nutshell statements and the highlighted profile bands may become a helpful framework for conducting a parent–teacher conference, especially if the teacher has a collection of work samples, exemplifying the profile comments, to share with the parent.

At the end of one school year or before school starts the next fall, profiles form an excellent basis for consultation between the 'ending' teacher and the 'receiving' teacher. Since the profile is based on evidence — observation and accompanying work samples — there is little danger that teachers are merely handing on their own prejudices regarding specific students, a problem that exists all too often when 'teacher comments' are passed along without the more objective profile data.

Such information may be particularly valuable when the student has been assigned to brief summer-school experience in order to remediate a failure to achieve desired outcomes. The more explicit information in a profile can be used to tailor that summer-school experience to fit the needs of the student. And since growth may be slight in a six-week period, the fact the several more behaviors on the band have now been highlighted may be the most valid way to describe growth over the summer.

When several teachers of a given grade all use profiles and are able to combine the insights into the growth of students in their grade level that the profiles provide, they may conclude that there needs to be some change in their curriculum outline, in the materials they use, or in the instructional strategies they are adopting. The profiles thus provide a framework for continuing curriculum design by the teachers themselves.

At this point, it would be well to reassert that literacy profiles are useful in charting the growth of *all* students, including those who might be described as academically gifted, those who are in need of remedial instruction, and those with other identified special needs.

Most funded programs in the United States still require norm-referenced testing as documentation of student growth, although changes are beginning in that regard. However, even though identification and evaluation of growth in programs such as Title I may have to remain norm-referenced, the use of profile information can pinpoint specific needs of students who may all be 'below the 23rd percentile' but are not in any other ways identical. Thus, profiles may help to shape remediation in the same ways that they are useful in other classroom planning situations.

One of the greatest strengths of the profiles is that their descriptions of literacy behaviors are not tied to specific age or grade cohorts. Thus, they may be particularly helpful in monitoring the performance of individuals whose growth is very atypical of their chronological age or grade placement. This aspect of profile use is discussed at greater length in chapter 11.

For the most part, profiles are completed by teachers who have first-hand evidence, by observation and work sample, that the student has exhibited the relevant behaviors. And there is significant evidence that parental observation of 'at home' behaviors may not tally completely with teachers' observations of 'at school' behaviors. There are times, however, when teachers or other school staff may wish to use the framework of the profile bands to elicit information from parents or other caregivers about a child's current literacy status in order to provide a starting point for further assessment.

For example, young children first entering school arrive with widely varying literacy experiences in the home. Also, some have had extensive preschool experience, while others have had none. Use of the profiles as part of the screening process when these children enter school may be an effective way of beginning a dialogue with parents about their children's progress, as well as a way of identifying individual patterns of literacy and instructional need. With older children entering the building for the first time, the profiles can also be extremely useful as an adjunct to records coming from the sending school, as well as a talking point with parents new to the system.

From the parents' point of view, the profiles provide a way for school staff to communicate with them without resorting to jargon or educationese on the one hand or to difficult-to-understand scores or statistical data on the other. Further, the profile descriptions may make it easier for parents to participate in their children's learning and to look for the next steps in their growth.

From the point of view of the school administration, profiles may be of great value in focusing the attention of the faculty, parents, and school board on needed changes in curriculum design and delivery, as well as on issues of standard-setting and monitoring of change. Aggregated profiles are also helpful to building teams in site-based shared decision making and as a vehicle for addressing instructional reform, both at the building and the district level. (See section 3 for more detailed descriptions of such reporting procedures.)

## A bit of history

Profiles were developed to satisfy a need for more detailed descriptions of student learning. In a research project that lasted for four years, from 1986 to 1989, more than 140 teachers were involved in observing students in literacy learning situations ranging from Grade 1 to Grade 12. They were asked to monitor growth in and to document the indicators of reading, writing and spoken language behavior. The indicators of growth were then used in a series of student surveys to develop scales of growth. Thousands of students were observed and the resulting data used to scale the indicators.

The full list of indicators was examined for patterns that might be useful in summarising the indicators into bands. Several patterns were evident in the list of calibrated indicators of reading and writing behavior. The progressions seemed to be related to underlying factors such as *attitudinal behavior, influence of reading on writing, role playing, retelling behavior, reactions to reading materials, analysis and interpretation, social or interactive roles in reading behavior, word approach skills, types of reading materials used* and so on. Nine bands were developed for each of reading, writing and spoken language. The number of bands, however, does not represent anything other than the apparent groupings of indicators. In fact, the original form of the reading and writing scales had seven bands, but there was a tendency to interpret the seven levels as consistent with the seven grades in a K–6 system. The project team reconstituted the teacher groups, added teachers from Grades 7–12 and then deliberately developed nine bands to avoid the correspondence with grade levels, setting band A as the earliest developmental level.

Teachers and language consultants have been consulted in several countries. The band scales were distributed to teachers and to sample groups of academics, consultants, and inspectors and other advisers in several Australian states, in the United States, New Zealand, Ireland, and the United Kingdom. They were asked to act as 'expert informants', to review the draft version of the bands and to advise on the need to edit, delete or move the indicators included in the bands or (if they considered that important indicators of the development of reading were missing) to suggest additional indicators. Advice was also sought on the structure, appropriate use and suitability of the band scales.

The profiles therefore describe indications of increasing achievement. Early levels of achievement are described in terms of beginning skills, knowledge, and concepts; the bands then progress to outline more advanced skills, deeper knowledge, and more sophisticated understandings.

The bands are meant to form a quasi-cumulative scale; that is, a student placed at band E is likely to have behavior patterns indicated by bands A, B, C and D as well as some behaviors in band E. It is not obligatory that every student exhibit all behaviors in each band. Teachers report that holistic impressions allow them to judge whether a student is beyond a band level, has not yet reached that level, or is developing the behaviors indicated at the level. Different interpretations of development were also possible. Some teachers felt more comfortable discriminating between students who were just beginning to exhibit the behaviors in a level and those who were well into it but had not completely developed the level of competence.

This interpretation of student progress was later adopted for more formal survey work during the field trials.

Data from pilot studies with the profiles provided firm support for their cumulative nature. In general, students who are rated as having established the behaviors in a particular band have already established those described in preceding bands. However, the bands are far from a stepwise sequence of development and they are not equivalent in length.

**SECTION 2**

# Building profiles

# CHAPTER 3

# Getting started

Unlike a test score, which may be quick to obtain, a literacy profile takes a little time to build at first because it is complex and rich in information. This does not mean, however, that profile building has to be arduous. After a while it may become second nature to teachers and take very little time at all. It is, after all, an articulation of what teachers see and do in ordinary, everyday classrooms. Recording information about students' learning should be a simple and routine part of teaching and learning when a teacher gets into the habit of recording significant observations and judgments and when a system is provided that enables the recordings to be easily made. The literacy profiles provide such a system.

The profiles are a kind of short cut to the use of detailed anecdotal records. By presenting descriptions of typical classroom behaviors, they offer a useful observation format that requires little more than some notes or jottings about the context of the observation and any other relevant information the teacher may wish to include. Frequent but brief entries made over a whole year can build a comprehensive profile and a comprehensive component of a portfolio. The product of this operation can then be both a record of progress monitored and a report on the student.

The items listed in the bands of the profiles are not meant to be checked off one by one. The bands do not constitute a checklist; rather, they are to be read as a cluster of typical behaviors that the teacher judges to be either present or not. As experience in using them grows, teachers will gain a feeling for the typical behaviors in each of the bands.

One might, for instance, think, 'The way Christopher talks about his reading of narrative suggests band D to me. Yet his very tentative following of instructions in this technical prose is clearly Band C'. Such familiarity with the bands will only come gradually, but it can be achieved; hundreds of teachers, while working on the development of the profiles, have demonstrated that it can be done without too much difficulty. Moreover, after a while teachers find the nutshell — which captures the gist of the level — more useful than the detail of the band.

The teacher is not alone in profile building. Other staff members, including the librarian, have contributions to make. But there are further participants in assessment who can become committed to the collection of evidence as well: these are the students themselves and their parents. If their contribution is to be positive, they must know what to look for and how to store the information they find. Students can keep a reading log, for example, a homework log, and selected work samples as evidence of growth. Parents can record aspects of development in literacy, new interests developed and any literacy tasks worked on. Such data should ultimately be reflected on the literacy profiles record.

## Profile building in practise

It is important that profile building draws on a variety of learning contexts, extends over a long period and is complemented by samples of students' work maintained in a portfolio. Judgments about students should always relate to some tangible evidence.

Profile building could involve the teacher in the following way.

### Daily
Writing a note or comment on the records of two or three students in each class.

### Weekly
Choosing two or three students in each class and making a formal judgment about their progress through the reading and writing bands.

### Each school term
Making a systematic review and update of the judgments made for each student. Perhaps, with each one, spending a few minutes going over the written work kept in the writing folder or talking about the student's comments in the reading log. Also recording relevant information gathered from parent–teacher meetings or interviews.

By the end of each term the teacher should be able to talk about every student, pointing to specific items in the relevant bands, indicating the context in which the judgments were made and illustrating the decision with materials from the portfolio.

## Understanding the layout

The layout of the profile record sheets in chapters 4 to 8 has been described in chapter 1. Taking writing band E as an example, the nutshell statement is given first on the left-hand page.

> **Can plan, organize and polish writing. Writes in paragraphs. Vocabulary and grammar are suited to the topic. Can write convincing stories.**

Below this are descriptions of common classroom tasks and contexts within which teachers might make their observations—for example, writing circles.

> **Writing circles** provide occasions for teacher and peers to assist cohesion, structure and appropriate use of tense, number and person.

On the right-hand page is the profiles record, where band E of writing behaviors is displayed together with the preceding and following bands, shown in a smaller typeface as is shown in the example on page 5.

Note that the profiles for viewing and listening, as has been mentioned, are still in the development stage. For this reason, the detail of assessment contexts is still being evolved. Perhaps teachers who use these scales would be able in the future to contribute to the contexts.

## Preparation for use in the classroom

For children first entering school, the classroom teacher might photocopy the records labelled Reading band A, Writing band A and Spoken language band A so that they are available for all members of the class. On each one the student's name is written in the space provided. Before photocopying, the teacher can insert at the top of the sheet the name of the school and the particular class, together with the current year. Normally, these records will go to the teacher of the class in the following year. Succeeding records are added to each student's portfolio when and as required.

Teachers at other grade levels who are introducing the profiles for the first time will need to have some knowledge of their students before they can judge which is the most appropriate band to use. Some students may exhibit behaviors that spread over several bands, and thus will require two or more records.

## Using the profile record sheet

Imagine a kindergarten student at about Thanksgiving. The teacher decides to start building a reading profile for that student. One heading under Reading band A is 'Interests and attitudes'; the teacher might without hesitation put a check beside this, knowing that the student 'shows preference for particular books' and 'chooses books as a free time activity'. These are typical behaviors listed under this first heading. The teacher in this case would write in the expression 'Quiet reading time' to indicate the context in which the observation used in making this judgment took place, but might well have written 'Discussion with parents' or 'Reading conference', depending on the source of the information.

When looking at another heading, 'Concepts about print', the teacher might judge that the student in question still has a long way to go. The student might indeed 'hold the book the right way up', 'turn pages from the front to the back' and 'indicate the start and end of books', but might do so very hesitantly. The teacher might use a coloured highlighter pen to mark these behaviors on the record. There are many significant behaviors not yet indicated, however, and it is clear that the student is not confident enough with the basic concepts of print. There are several other typical behaviors that the teacher will look out for in the coming weeks and will perhaps mark them with a different-colored pen. A color can be used to show when the indicator was achieved. The change of color indicates the rate of progress as well as what the student is achieving.

Scanning the typical behaviors listed under 'Reading strategies', the teacher might judge that insufficient evidence of the suggested behaviors are displayed by the student and not record that these behaviors are demonstrated. For 'Responses', however, he or she may confidently check the heading and perhaps note 'Shared reading' in the comments column.

By spring, the teacher might have put a check beside each of the subheadings and can confidently check the major heading Reading band A. But by this time, of course, there might be a check beside the subheading 'Responses' in reading band B because the teacher has observed a significant number of behaviors appropriate to this level — some actually listed in Reading band B and others included by the teacher. In some cases the teacher recorded the date and the comment on the observation.

A record sheet filled out in this way serves as the basis for discussing progress with the student, the parents and other teachers, and also serves as the raw material from which the written report on literacy is prepared.

## Steps in building a student's literacy profile

- Choose three students in the class. They should represent widely different levels of literacy development.
- After you have looked at the nutshells, observe these students closely and mark on a record page (with a highlighter pen) those indicators that each student shows on a consistent basis.
- Choose a band that best describes the typical literacy behaviors of one student.
- Scan the bands on either side of the chosen one. Remember that the range of behaviors might spread over many bands.
- Photocopy an appropriate record for reading, writing and spoken language for each of the students being profiled.
- Write the student's name on each sheet, adding the school name, class and term.
- Look particularly at the statements describing typical behaviors within a band and make a judgment as to whether they describe in general the behavior of the student. If they do, check the heading for that group of descriptors, for example, 'What the writing shows'.
- Indicate in the comment column the date at which the judgment was made
- Jot down in the context of observation the particular task or context that was the source of the judgment.
- Note any comments that will help in an interview with parents, in writing a report or in the direction of future learning experiences.
- Place a check against a given band (for instance band B) once all the headings have been checked.
- Record details of other assessments as they become available. These might include additional information from parents or from student self-assessment.

- For other students in the class, observe and use the nutshell statements to determine where, approximately, they are on each of the profile scales. Check your estimates later by referring to the full listing of pointers in the full scales.
- Use the nutshell, then the detail.
- Decide whether for each band level, the students:
  - have not yet reached these behaviors;
  - are beginning to demonstrate them;
  - are developing a significant number of these behaviors;
  - are beyond this band level in their growth.
File the records in the students' portfolios.

Starting to use the profiles with only a small number of students and learning the detail with that small number makes the task of getting started much easier. Learning to focus on the nutshell statements before checking on the details in the lists also makes it easier to start profiling in the class. Before long, the content of the profiles becomes a natural extension of the teacher's language, and the detail becomes less important. The 'nutshell first' approach will help to make the profiles a natural part of the teacher's repertoire.

# CHAPTER 4
# Reading profile records

VIEWING

LISTENING

SPOKEN LANGUAGE

WRITING

READING

## Contexts for observation

A **reading conference**, during which the student talks with the teacher about a text the student has read, enables the teacher to observe the way the student handles books and to discover the student's responses, reading strategies and understandings about print.

**Shared reading** time provides an opportunity to observe students' responses to books and stories.

During **quiet reading** time, the teacher can observe each student's vocabulary reading behavior, and interest in and knowledge about books.

Discussion with **parents** can yield valuable information about the student's reading interests and behavior.

**Writing sessions** in the classroom provide opportunities for observing some of the ways

students show their understanding about print and its conventions.

Engagement with **other students'** work and **labels** can be further demonstrations of understandings about text.

**Practical sessions** (sand and water activities, construction, role play) also enable the teacher to observe durability of strategies in settings beyond reading.

Marie Clay's Sand and Stones tests and *The Early Detection of Reading Difficulties* (Heinemann, NH, 1985), can be used to identify what students know about the way print is organized.

**Oral cloze** exercises may indicate students' understandings of both semantic and syntactic knowledge.

I

H

G

F

E

D

C

B

A

School ............................................................ Class ........

Name ............................................................ Term .........

# Reading band A

**Concepts about print**

Holds book the right way up. Turns pages from front to back. On request, indicates the beginnings and ends of sentences. Distinguishes between upper- and lower-case letters. Indicates the start and end of a book.

**Reading strategies**

Locates words, lines, spaces, letters. Refers to letters by name. Locates own name and other familiar words in a short text. Identifies known, familiar words in other contexts.

**Responses**

Responds to literature (smiles, claps, listens intently). Joins in familiar stories.

**Interests and attitudes**

Shows preference for particular books. Chooses books as a free-time activity.

# Reading band B

COMMENT

**Reading strategies**

Takes risks when reading. 'Reads' books with simple, repetitive language patterns. 'Reads', understands and explains own 'writing'. Is aware that print tells a story. Uses pictures for clues to meaning of text. Asks others for help with meaning and pronunciation of words. Consistently reads familar words and interprets symbols within a text. Predicts words. Matches known clusters of letters to clusters in unknown words. Locates own name and other familiar words in a short text. Uses knowledge of words in the environment when 'reading' and 'writing'. Uses various strategies to follow a line of print. Copies classroom print, labels, signs, etc.

**Responses**

Selects own books to 'read'. Describes connections among events in texts. Writes, role-plays and/or draws in response to a story or other form of writing (e.g. poem, message). Creates ending when text is left unfinished. Recounts parts of text in writing, drama or artwork. Retells, using language expressions from reading sources. Retells with approximate sequence.

**Interests and attitudes**

Explores a variety of books. Begins to show an interest in specific type of literature. Plays at reading books. Talks about favorite books.

# Suggested new indicators

VIEWING

LISTENING

SPOKEN LANGUAGE

WRITING

READING

B C D E F G H I

A

VIEWING

LISTENING

SPOKEN LANGUAGE

WRITING

READING

A B C D E F G H I

## Contexts for observation

**Reading conferences** help the teacher to observe the strategies each student is using to reach understanding. During the conference, the teacher is able to discuss parts of a book, listen to the student read aloud from a familiar text, and introduce self-assessment procedures.

**Reading logs**, where the student or the teacher maintains a list of books the student has read, provide a record of development in reading. Reading logs may include some assessment of books read, as well as the students' assessment of their own reading.

**Shared reading** gives an indication of each student's recognition of language patterns and interpretation of symbols. Shared reading provides support for the less confident student.

**Retelling** of what has been read permits the teacher to make judgments about a student's understanding and to examine the effects reading has upon vocabulary and language structures. Reading may be expressed as art, drama, or writing as well as orally. Retelling of non-fiction as well as fiction material is valuable.

**Cloze** activities may show students' abilities in using graphophonemic, semantic and syntactic cues.

Classroom observations provide the basis for anecdotal records. Records of behaviors, as they are observed while **listening** to and **talking** with students, become significant when the collected information is considered over time, and patterns in development can be identified.

**Parent** discussions provide insights into a student's interest and involvement in reading outside school hours.

During **drama** activities, teachers can observe those students who are able to internalize characterization and meaning from text.

Stories can be cut up by the teacher and reassembled by the student. This enables the teacher to check on **sequencing** strategies employed by the student.

When students are **writing**, much can be observed regarding their knowledge of the purpose and conventions of print.

# Reading band A

COMMENT

## Concepts about print
Holds book the right way up. Turns pages from front to back. On request, indicates the beginnings and ends of sentences. Distinguishes between upper- and lower-case letters. Indicates the start and end of a book.

## Reading strategies
Locates words, lines, spaces, letters. Refers to letters by name. Locates own name and other familiar words in a short text. Identifies known, familiar words in other contexts.

## Responses
Responds to literature (smiles, claps, listens intently). Joins in familiar stories.

## Interests and attitudes
Shows preference for particular books. Chooses books as a free-time activity.

# Reading band B

COMMENT

## Reading strategies
Takes risks when reading. 'Reads' books with simple, repetitive language patterns. 'Reads', understands and explains own 'writing'. Is aware that print tells a story. Uses pictures for clues to meaning of text. Asks others for help with meaning and pronunciation of words. Consistently reads familar words and interprets symbols within a text. Predicts words. Matches known clusters of letters to clusters in unknown words. Locates own name and other familiar words in a short text. Uses knowledge of words in the environment when 'reading' and 'writing'. Uses various strategies to follow a line of print. Copies classroom print, labels, signs, etc.

## Responses
Selects own books to 'read'. Describes connections among events in texts. Writes, role-plays and/or draws in response to a story or other form of writing (e.g. poem, message). Creates ending when text is left unfinished. Recounts parts of text in writing, drama or artwork. Retells, using language expressions from reading sources. Retells with approximate sequence.

## Interests and attitudes
Explores a variety of books. Begins to show an interest in specific type of literature. Plays at reading books. Talks about favorite books.

# Reading band C

COMMENT

## Reading strategies
Rereads a paragraph or sentence to establish meaning. Uses context as a basis for predicting meaning of unfamiliar words. Reads aloud, showing understanding of purpose of punctuation marks. Uses picture cues to make appropriate responses for unknown words. Uses pictures to help read a text. Finds where another reader is up to in a reading passage.

## Responses
Writing and artwork reflect understanding of text. Retells, discusses and expresses opinions on literature, and reads further. Recalls events and characters spontaneously from text.

## Interests and attitudes
Seeks recommendations for books to read. Chooses more than one type of book. Chooses to read when given free choice. Concentrates on reading for lengthy periods.

# Suggested new indicators

**Reading band** **C** Looks for meaning in text. Reading and discussion of text shows enjoyment of reading. Shares experience with others.

## Contexts for observation

**Shared reading** sessions provide opportunities for teachers to observe how students read aloud, predict text and respond to meaning.

During the **reading conference**, students can be encouraged to read aloud from their selected books. The prior knowledge they have about the stories enables them to demonstrate their understanding of the function of punctuation marks.

**Reading logs** can be used by students to record their opinions about literature; as well, they give an indication of the type of material being read.

**Sustained silent reading** enables teachers to observe each student's engagement with text over increasing periods.

**Retelling** provides a guide to assessing each student's recall of details, and also provides information about the cues being used. These may be oral, written, in role play, through art or in responding to and acting upon what has been read.

**Running records** are of assistance when there are concerns about specific students. A number of these should be taken over a period and compared to give an indication of individual students' strengths and weaknesses in reading. Be sure to assess comprehension as well as fluency.

**Observation** and **anecdotal records** provide cumulative data about development in reading and writing.

**Cloze activities** enable observation of how students use cueing systems in reading.

**Parents** have much to offer about students' reading, and so regular discussions should be arranged.

As students read aloud from familiar text during **readers' theater** (that is, dramatized reading), the teacher is able to observe and assess use of voice and understandings about the purpose of punctuation.

**Sharing sessions** are times when students are able to·seek and make recommendations for books to read.

Creative **drama** will show how students individually interpret text in different situations.

# Reading band B

COMMENT

### Reading strategies

Takes risks when reading. 'Reads' books with simple, repetitive language patterns. 'Reads', understands and explains own 'writing'. Is aware that print tells a story. Uses pictures for clues to meaning of text. Asks others for help with meaning and pronunciation of words. Consistently reads familar words and interprets symbols within a text. Predicts words. Matches known clusters of letters to clusters in unknown words. Locates own name and other familiar words in a short text. Uses knowledge of words in the environment when 'reading' and 'writing'. Uses various strategies to follow a line of print. Copies classroom print, labels, signs, etc.

### Responses

Selects own books to 'read'. Describes connections among events in texts. Writes, role-plays and/or draws in response to a story or other form of writing (e.g. poem, message). Creates ending when text is left unfinished. Recounts parts of text in writing, drama or artwork. Retells, using language expressions from reading sources. Retells with approximate sequence.

### Interests and attitudes

Explores a variety of books. Begins to show an interest in specific type of literature. Plays at reading books. Talks about favorite books.

# Reading band C

COMMENT

### Reading strategies

Rereads a paragraph or sentence to establish meaning. Uses context as a basis for predicting meaning of unfamiliar words. Reads aloud, showing understanding of purpose of punctuation marks. Uses picture cues to make appropriate responses for unknown words. Uses pictures to help read a text. Finds where another reader is up to in a reading passage.

### Responses

Writing and artwork reflect understanding of text. Retells, discusses and expresses opinions on literature, and reads further. Recalls events and characters spontaneously from text.

### Interests and attitudes

Seeks recommendations for books to read. Chooses more than one type of book. Chooses to read when given free choice. Concentrates on reading for lengthy periods.

# Reading band D

COMMENT

### Reading strategies

Reads material with a wide variety of styles and topics. Selects books to fulfil own purposes. States main idea in a passage. Substitutes words with similar meanings when reading aloud. Self-corrects, using knowledge of language structure and sound–symbol relationships. Predicts, using knowledge of language structure and/or sound/symbol to make sense of a word or a phrase.

### Responses

Discusses different types of reading materials. Discusses materials read at home. Tells a variety of audiences about a book. Uses vocabulary and sentence structure from reading materials in written work as well as in conversation. Uses themes from reading in artwork. Follows written instructions.

### Interests and attitudes

Recommends books to others. Reads often. Reads silently for extended periods.

# Suggested new indicators

VIEWING

LISTENING

SPOKEN LANGUAGE

WRITING

READING

A B C D E F G H I

**Reading band** **D**

Expects and anticipates sense and meaning in text. Discussion reflects grasp of whole meanings. Now absorbs ideas and language.

VIEWING

LISTENING

SPOKEN LANGUAGE

WRITING

READING

A B C D E F G H I

## Contexts for observation

**Reading circles**, where each student discusses a chosen book with peers, provide opportunities to share different types of reading materials with a variety of audiences. Some forms of peer conferencing may take place at these.

**Sustained silent reading** permits students to read books of their own choice for extended periods without interruption.

**Reading logs** may be simply a list of books read or may become a vehicle wherein students critically review the books they have read and assess their own growth in reading.

Discussions with **parents** about a student's out-of-school reading habits can be useful, as can teacher–child conferences. During these times the variety of reading materials chosen, plus interests and general development, can be noted and added to observational records. Prior discussions can provide clues as to the student's ability to make predictions about books, and give an insight into how books are selected.

When progress in reading appears to be slow, **miscue analysis** can be used to ascertain which parts of the process are being inefficiently used and/or relied upon.

Activities in **controlled cloze** allow for the recording of strengths and problems students encounter.

**Role playing** will allow students to explore characterizations in different settings. Drama enables them to demonstrate their depth of textual understanding.

**Activities** within the classroom provide many opportunities to observe students following directions. These range from making models, playing board games and cooking through to following instructions using the computer.

**Portfolios** of students' work in writing, art, reading and other areas are valuable records of development, and examination of these enables growth to be monitored closely. It is important that work in portfolios is dated where possible.

**Reading profile record**

School ........................................................ Class ........
Name ........................................................ Term .........

# Reading band C

COMMENT

### Reading strategies
Rereads a paragraph or sentence to establish meaning. Uses context as a basis for predicting meaning of unfamiliar words. Reads aloud, showing understanding of purpose of punctuation marks. Uses picture cues to make appropriate responses for unknown words. Uses pictures to help read a text. Finds where another reader is up to in a reading passage.

### Responses
Writing and artwork reflect understanding of text. Retells, discusses and expresses opinions on literature, and reads further. Recalls events and characters spontaneously from text.

### Interests and attitudes
Seeks recommendations for books to read. Chooses more than one type of book. Chooses to read when given free choice. Concentrates on reading for lengthy periods.

# Reading band D

COMMENT

### Reading strategies
Reads material with a wide variety of styles and topics. Selects books to fulfil own purposes. States main idea in a passage. Substitutes words with similar meanings when reading aloud. Self-corrects, using knowledge of language structure and sound–symbol relationships. Predicts, using knowledge of language structure and/or sound/symbol to make sense of a word or a phrase.

### Responses
Discusses different types of reading materials. Discusses materials read at home. Tells a variety of audiences about a book. Uses vocabulary and sentence structure from reading materials in written work as well as in conversation. Uses themes from reading in artwork. Follows written instructions.

### Interests and attitudes
Recommends books to others. Reads often. Reads silently for extended periods.

# Reading band E

COMMENT

### Reading strategies
Reads to others with few inappropriate pauses. Interprets new words by reference to suffixes, prefixes and meaning of word parts. Uses directories such as a table of contents or an index, or telephone and street directories, to locate information. Uses library classification systems to find specific reading materials.

### Responses
Improvises in role play, drawing on a range of text. Writing shows meaning inferred from the text. Explains a piece of literature. Expresses and supports an opinion on whether an author's point of view is valid. Discusses implied motives of characters in the text. Makes comments and expresses feelings about characters. Rewrites information from text in own words. Uses text as a model for own writing. Uses a range of books and print materials as information sources for written work. Reads aloud with expression.

# Suggested new indicators

VIEWING

LISTENING

SPOKEN LANGUAGE

WRITING

READING

A B C D E F G H I

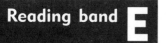
VIEWING

LISTENING

SPOKEN LANGUAGE

WRITING

**READING**

I

H

G

F

**E**

D

C

B

A

## Contexts for observation

**Reading logs** will show the variety and types of material being read for information or pleasure and demonstrate the effect upon each student's writing. These are useful guides to progress, and may be coupled with some form of literature-response journal where students reflect upon text — about, between and beyond what is read — and assess their own development.

**Reading circles** supply varied audiences for students' views about books. Teachers and peers are able to ask detailed and probing questions regarding character, plot and setting. Readers' feelings and opinions may be explored.

**Portfolios**, which reflect reading experiences, are important measures of development. Themes recurrent in reading may appear in writing and even in artwork.

**Practical demonstrations** and **projects** are also indications of growth in reading. Research

work and the interpretation of information will be seen in the presentation of projects. Model making and experiments may also show this.

Observation of students' **reading** as they work permits the teacher to record significant moments that should be recorded and dated.

Observing behaviors when students are engaged in **possible sentences** can also provide clues as to strategies employed to process print.

**Retelling** is another means through which students are able to express their understandings about text. Recall of details can be checked this way.

**Drama** activities give opportunities to observe student responses to what has been read and inferences from texts.

**Cooperative cloze** indicates whether students are able to manipulate text to satisfy the group.

**Reading profile record**

School ............................................................ Class ........
Name ............................................................ Term ........

# Reading band D

COMMENT

### Reading strategies

Reads material with a wide variety of styles and topics. Selects books to fulfil own purposes. States main idea in a passage. Substitutes words with similar meanings when reading aloud. Self-corrects, using knowledge of language structure and sound–symbol relationships. Predicts, using knowledge of language structure and/ or sound/symbol to make sense of a word or a phrase.

### Responses

Discusses different types of reading materials. Discusses materials read at home. Tells a variety of audiences about a book. Uses vocabulary and sentence structure from reading materials in written work as well as in conversation. Uses themes from reading in artwork. Follows written instructions.

### Interests and attitudes

Recommends books to others. Reads often. Reads silently for extended periods.

# Reading band E

COMMENT

### Reading strategies

Reads to others with few inappropriate pauses. Interprets new words by reference to suffixes, prefixes and meaning of word parts. Uses directories such as a table of contents or an index, or telephone and street directories, to locate information. Uses library classification systems to find specific reading materials.

### Responses

Improvises in role play, drawing on a range of text. Writing shows meaning inferred from the text. Explains a piece of literature. Expresses and supports an opinion on whether an author's point of view is valid. Discusses implied motives of characters in the text. Makes comments and expresses feelings about characters. Rewrites information from text in own words. Uses text as a model for own writing. Uses a range of books and print materials as information sources for written work. Reads aloud with expression.

# Reading band F

COMMENT

### Reading strategies

Describes links between personal experience and arguments and ideas in text. Selects relevant passages or phrases to answer questions without necessarily reading whole text. Formulates research topics and questions and finds relevant information from reading materials. Maps out plots and character developments in novels and other literary texts. Varies reading strategies according to purposes for reading and nature of text. Makes connections between texts, recognising similarities of themes and values.

### Responses

Discusses author's intent for the reader. Discusses styles used by different authors. Describes settings in literature. Forms generalizations about a range of genres, including myth, short story. Offers reasons for the feelings provoked by a text. Writing and discussions acknowledge a range of interpretations of text. Offers critical opinion or analysis of reading passages in discussion. Justifies own appraisal of a text. Synthesizes and expands on information from a range of texts in written work.

# Suggested new indicators

VIEWING

LISTENING

SPOKEN LANGUAGE

WRITING

**READING**

A B C D **E** F G H I

## Contexts for observation

**Reading circles** assume great importance, as they enable teachers and peers to jointly explore texts. Discussions about style, intent, response, opinions, analysis and generalizations can be examined closely and justified by reference to the book in question.

Maintenance of **reading logs** and **literature–learning journals** is vital, for it is here that the quality of reading materials is recorded. Students will be increasingly able to reflect upon their experiences, and to assess their own growth.

**Read and retell** is a method of closely examining the effects of a particular text. In this, students discuss possible contents of a passage from reading only the title, write their predictions and share them, then read the text. After a number of readings, students complete a written retelling of the passage and then compare this with the original. These retellings can be assessed by the teacher.

**Big cloze** enables observation to be made of students who are able to reconstruct 'chunks' of text based upon both prior and new knowledge of text structures.

Observations of **reading** enable the teacher to note how students process print, whether rate of reading is adjusted according to the purpose, what strategies are employed and whether these are appropriate. The records kept from these form the basis of anecdotal reporting.

Participating in **readers' theater** encourages students to read aloud with fluency and expression. Drama is a way of observing each student's personal responses, interpretations and understanding of non-fiction materials.

**Portfolios** from other subject areas assume increasing importance, as these demonstrate each student's ability to locate and use information from texts. Practical demonstrations/projects also provide information about this, and synthesis from a variety of sources can be evident in these.

**Reading profile record**

School ........................................................ Class ........
Name ........................................................ Term ........

# Reading band E

COMMENT

### Reading strategies

Reads to others with few inappropriate pauses. Interprets new words by reference to suffixes, prefixes and meaning of word parts. Uses directories such as a table of contents or an index, or telephone and street directories, to locate information. Uses library classification systems to find specific reading materials.

### Responses

Improvises in role play, drawing on a range of text. Writing shows meaning inferred from the text. Explains a piece of literature. Expresses and supports an opinion on whether an author's point of view is valid. Discusses implied motives of characters in the text. Makes comments and expresses feelings about characters. Rewrites information from text in own words. Uses text as a model for own writing. Uses a range of books and print materials as information sources for written work. Reads aloud with expression.

# Reading band F

COMMENT

### Reading strategies

Describes links between personal experience and arguments and ideas in text. Selects relevant passages or phrases to answer questions without necessarily reading whole text. Formulates research topics and questions and finds relevant information from reading materials. Maps out plots and character developments in novels and other literary texts. Varies reading strategies according to purposes for reading and nature of text. Makes connections between texts, recognising similarities of themes and values.

### Responses

Discusses author's intent for the reader. Discusses styles used by different authors. Describes settings in literature. Forms generalizations about a range of genres, including myth, short story. Offers reasons for the feelings provoked by a text. Writing and discussions acknowledge a range of interpretations of text. Offers critical opinion or analysis of reading passages in discussion. Justifies own appraisal of a text. Synthesizes and expands on information from a range of texts in written work.

# Reading band G

COMMENT

### Reading strategies

Reads manuals and literature of varying complexity. Interprets simple maps, tables and graphs in the context of discursive text. Makes generalizations and draws conclusions from reading. Reads at different speeds, using scanning, skim-reading or careful reading as appropriate.

### Responses

Supports argument or opinion by reference to evidence presented in sources outside text. Compares information from different sources. Identifies opposing points of view and main and supporting arguments in text. Comments on cohesiveness of text as a whole. Discusses and writes about author's bias and technique. In writing, offers critical opinion or analysis of reading materials. Distils and links ideas from complex sentences and paragraphs.

### Interests and attitudes

Reads widely for pleasure, for interest or for learning.

# Suggested new indicators

VIEWING

LISTENING

SPOKEN LANGUAGE

WRITING

READING

A B C D E F G H I

Reads for learning as well as pleasure. Reads widely and draws ideas and issues together. Is developing a critical approach to analysis of ideas and writing.

## Contexts for observation

Critical appraisal of works being read can be explored in **reading circles** — plot, character, bias, validity, and author's style are just some of the areas that can be discussed with peers and teachers. Personal responses and interpretation can also be shared.

**Learning journals**, **reading logs** and **portfolios** of work from all subject areas will provide information about each student's reading. These should be considered together to obtain a clearer picture of development.

**Practical demonstrations/projects** will show how information from a variety of sources is incorporated into completion of different tasks. This will, additionally, be a guide to the way opinions are supported. In conjunction with work portfolios, demonstrations and projects are real

evidence of a student's growth in processing expository text.

Individual interpretation of knowledge gained may be expressed through **drama**.

As well as assisting students to develop a critical awareness of reading materials. **Three-level guide** activities will provide an indication of each student's ability to support arguments with reference to text, to make generalizations and draw conclusions. Observation of **discussions** during these sessions will form a part of anecdotal records.

**Possible sentences** are also useful in assessing a student's processing of print.

**Argumentative writing** will demonstrate conclusions students have reached from their reading.

School ........................................................ Class ........

Name ........................................................ Term.........

# Reading band F

COMMENT

### Reading strategies

Describes links between personal experience and arguments and ideas in text. Selects relevant passages or phrases to answer questions without necessarily reading whole text. Formulates research topics and questions and finds relevant information from reading materials. Maps out plots and character developments in novels and other literary texts. Varies reading strategies according to purposes for reading and nature of text. Makes connections between texts, recognising similarities of themes and values.

### Responses

Discusses author's intent for the reader. Discusses styles used by different authors. Describes settings in literature. Forms generalizations about a range of genres, including myth, short story. Offers reasons for the feelings provoked by a text. Writing and discussions acknowledge a range of interpretations of text. Offers critical opinion or analysis of reading passages in discussion. Justifies own appraisal of a text. Synthesizes and expands on information from a range of texts in written work.

# Reading band G

COMMENT

### Reading strategies

Reads manuals and literature of varying complexity. Interprets simple maps, tables and graphs in the context of discursive text. Makes generalizations and draws conclusions from reading. Reads at different speeds, using scanning, skim-reading or careful reading as appropriate.

### Responses

Supports argument or opinion by reference to evidence presented in sources outside text. Compares information from different sources. Identifies opposing points of view and main and supporting arguments in text. Comments on cohesiveness of text as a whole. Discusses and writes about author's bias and technique. In writing, offers critical opinion or analysis of reading materials. Distils and links ideas from complex sentences and paragraphs.

### Interests and attitudes

Reads widely for pleasure, for interest or for learning.

# Reading band H

COMMENT

### Reading strategies

Compiles own list of needed references, using bibliographies and literature-search techniques. Interprets material at different levels of meaning. Forms generalizations about a range of genres, including myth, short story. Lists a wide variety of sources read for specific learning tasks.

### Responses

Identifies plot and subplot. Identifies allegory. Formulates hypothetical questions about a subject, based on prior reading. Compares and offers critical analysis of materials presented in the media. Extracts ideas embedded in complex passages of text. Displays critical opinion and analysis in written reports of reading. Identifies different authors' points of view on a topic. Reformulates a task in the light of available reading resources. Questions and reflects on issues encountered in texts. Shows understanding by being able to adopt an alternative point of view to the author's. Discusses styles used by different authors.

# Suggested new indicators

VIEWING · LISTENING · SPOKEN LANGUAGE · WRITING · READING

A B C D E F G H I

VIEWING

LISTENING

SPOKEN LANGUAGE

WRITING

READING

## Contexts for observation

**Reading circles** provide opportunities for students to discuss their interpretations of text at varying levels of meaning, to discuss styles used by authors, extract embedded ideas and identify authors' points of view. The interaction between teacher and students at reading circles can enhance and expand understandings about text.

**Practical demonstrations/projects** will permit the teacher to assess each student's ability to analyze media materials, reformulate tasks after considering available resources and compile appropriate reference lists.

Students' own **writing** will be an enduring artefact that will provide evidence of a variety of responses to and interpretations of text. Justification of ideas encountered in reading will also be evident, as will understanding of authors' social comment.

Students' personal **literature response** and **learning journals**, plus written work from all curriculum areas, provide a summary of achievement recorded over time. The variety and type of materials being read, plus critical reports and analyses, are contained within these, as are the lists of sources used for specific learning tasks and reflections upon issues encountered in texts.

Development of **preview questions** or a set of **subheadings** for notes before reading a chapter or book gives information about the way students use their prior knowledge to predict what they expect to find in a text.

**Reading profile record**

School ........................................................ Class ........
Name ........................................................ Term ........

# Reading band G

COMMENT

### Reading strategies
Reads manuals and literature of varying complexity. Interprets simple maps, tables and graphs in the context of discursive text. Makes generalizations and draws conclusions from reading. Reads at different speeds, using scanning, skim-reading or careful reading as appropriate.

### Responses
Supports argument or opinion by reference to evidence presented in sources outside text. Compares information from different sources. Identifies opposing points of view and main and supporting arguments in text. Comments on cohesiveness of text as a whole. Discusses and writes about author's bias and technique. In writing, offers critical opinion or analysis of reading materials. Distils and links ideas from complex sentences and paragraphs.

### Interests and attitudes
Reads widely for pleasure, for interest or for learning.

# Reading band H

COMMENT

### Reading strategies
Compiles own list of needed references, using bibliographies and literature-search techniques. Interprets material at different levels of meaning. Forms generalizations about a range of genres, including myth, short story. Lists a wide variety of sources read for specific learning tasks.

### Responses
Identifies plot and subplot. Identifies allegory. Formulates hypothetical questions about a subject, based on prior reading. Compares and offers critical analysis of materials presented in the media. Extracts ideas embedded in complex passages of text. Displays critical opinion and analysis in written reports of reading. Identifies different authors' points of view on a topic. Reformulates a task in the light of available reading resources. Questions and reflects on issues encountered in texts. Shows understanding by being able to adopt an alternative point of view to the author's. Discusses styles used by different authors.

# Reading band I

COMMENT

### Reading strategies
Examines situational meaning of text. Explores a range of meaning dependent on the combination of influences of writer, reader and situation.

### Responses
Explains textual innuendo and undertone. Interprets analogy, allegory and parable in text. Identifies and explains deeper significance in text. Defends each interpretation of text. Discusses and writes about author's bias. Analyzes cohesiveness of text as a whole.

# Suggested new indicators

VIEWING
LISTENING
SPOKEN LANGUAGE
WRITING
READING
I
H
G
F
E
D
C
B
A

VIEWING LISTENING SPOKEN LANGUAGE WRITING READING

I H G F E D C B A

## Contexts for observation

Discussion of issues at **reading circles** provides opportunities for students to share issues of significance. These should then be explored through texts that focus on interpretation, authors' bias, innuendo and undertone.

**Literature response portfolios** provide a vehicle for students to critically and analytically consider text. Negotiated criteria will determine the direction student responses take. These criteria should be listed in the portfolio.

**Discussion** with students about **text cohesion** will allow the teacher to observe how well they make interpretations and justify decisions. Students' understanding regarding the cultural milieu of novels may be elicited here.

**Drama workshop**, in which students rehearse and revise their interpretations of a scene from a play, provides an occasion for observing the way students articulate and defend their perceptions of a text.

**Writing** and **discussion** reveal students' understandings about the way a literary work may be both a particular story and a more general illumination of aspects of human life.

**Close analysis** of a selected passage and the ways in which it relates to and illuminates the whole work will show students' understanding of structural and metaphoric cohesion in the text.

# Reading band H

COMMENT

## Reading strategies

Compiles own list of needed references, using bibliographies and literature-search techniques. Interprets material at different levels of meaning. Forms generalizations about a range of genres, including myth, short story. Lists a wide variety of sources read for specific learning tasks.

## Responses

Identifies plot and sub-plot. Identifies allegory. Formulates hypothetical questions about a subject, based on prior reading. Compares and offers critical analysis of materials presented in the media. Extracts ideas embedded in complex passages of text. Displays critical opinion and analysis in written reports of reading. Identifies different authors' points of view on a topic. Reformulates a task in the light of available reading resources. Questions and reflects on issues encountered in texts. Shows understanding by being able to adopt an alternative point of view to the author's. Discusses styles used by different authors.

# Reading band I

COMMENT

## Reading strategies

Examines situational meaning of text. Explores a range of meaning dependent on the combination of influences of writer, reader and situation.

## Responses

Explains textual innuendo and undertone. Interprets analogy, allegory and parable in text. Identifies and explains deeper significance in text. Defends each interpretation of text. Discusses and writes about author's bias. Analyzes cohesiveness of text as a whole.

# Suggested new indicators

VIEWING

LISTENING

SPOKEN LANGUAGE

WRITING

READING

A B C D E F G H I

**CHAPTER 5**
# Writing profile records

## Contexts for observation

A **writing conference**, during which students talk with the teacher about what has been written and/or drawn, enables the teacher to discover the strategies students are using to record their messages. Choice of writing implement and paper will also be apparent. Writing conferences allow students to reread their writing and/or drawing, and thus enable the teacher to note how each one approaches the notion of 'recording a message over time'.

During **writing sessions**, the teacher is able to observe each student's preference in the selection of different writing instruments and paper. This may suggest something of his or her previous writing experience. Each student's control over the use of writing implements, and embryonic control over some of the conventions of writing — recognizable symbols, letters, drawings and the use made of words copied from the classroom or school environment — will all be evident during these times.

**Discussion with parents** can provide further information about the student's experiences with writing and drawing.

**Writing profile record**

School ........................................................... Class ........
Name ............................................................ Term ........

# Writing band A

COMMENT

### What the writer does
Uses writing implement to make marks on paper. Explains the meaning of marks (word, sentence, writing, letter). Copies 'words' from signs in immediate environment. 'Reads', understands and explains own 'writing'.

### What the writing shows
Understanding of the difference between picture and print. Use of some recognizable symbols in writing.

### Use of writing
Comments on signs and other symbols in immediate environment. Uses a mixture of drawings and 'writing' to convey and support an idea.

# Writing band B

COMMENT

### What the writer does
Reproduces words from signs and other sources in immediate environment. Holds pencil/pen using satisfactory grip. Uses preferred hand consistently for writing. Attempts to put 'words' in 'sentence' format. 'Writes' a simple message. Uses sound–symbol linkages. 'Captions' or 'labels' drawings.

### What the writing shows
Use of vocabulary of print (letters, words, question marks, etc.). Use of letters of the alphabet and other conventional symbols. Use of letters in groups to form words. Placing of spaces between groups of 'letters'. Knowledge that writing moves from left to right in lines from top to bottom of page.

### Use of writing
Writes own name.

### Interests and attitudes
Understands that writing is talk written down.

# Suggested new indicators

VIEWING

LISTENING

SPOKEN LANGUAGE

WRITING

READING

I H G F E D C B A

Is learning about handwriting. Knows what letters and words are and can talk about ideas in own writing. Is starting to write recognizable letters and words.

## Contexts for observation

Observation of students during **writing sessions** allows the teacher to continue to monitor increasing control and preference of hand and writing implements. Developing understandings about the conventions of print will also be apparent, and for each student these should be noted, with dates, for records.

The **writing conference** is an opportunity for students to talk with teachers about their writing. This may take the form of 'reading' what has been written or discussing the writing and/or drawing. Such times are rich sources of information and reveal much about students' understandings of the conventions and vocabulary of print and about the meaning they are making in their writing.

From **samples** in the **writing folio,** teachers will be able to identify student development in the use of writing conventions, and the range of ideas and vocabulary in use. The writing folio itself may be used to develop ideas for writing, as well as a list of the language conventions they are employing. This enables the teacher to locate quickly students who need assistance with ideas for writing, and also to celebrate achievements with their students.

**Shared reading** sessions are times when students are able to share their developing knowledge of the vocabulary of print and to question those elements that are engaging their attention. Observant teachers will increase their knowledge about students during shared reading.

# Writing band A

COMMENT

### What the writer does
Uses writing implement to make marks on paper. Explains the meaning of marks (word, sentence, writing, letter). Copies 'words' from signs in immediate environment. 'Reads', understands and explains own 'writing'.

### What the writing shows
Understanding of the difference between picture and print. Use of some recognizable symbols in writing.

### Use of writing
Comments on signs and other symbols in immediate environment. Uses a mixture of drawings and 'writing' to convey and support an idea.

# Writing band B

COMMENT

### What the writer does
Reproduces words from signs and other sources in immediate environment. Holds pencil/pen using satisfactory grip. Uses preferred hand consistently for writing. Attempts to put 'words' in 'sentence' format. 'Writes' a simple message. Uses sound–symbol linkages. 'Captions' or 'labels' drawings.

### What the writing shows
Use of vocabulary of print (letters, words, question marks, etc.). Use of letters of the alphabet and other conventional symbols. Use of letters in groups to form words. Placing of spaces between groups of 'letters'. Knowledge that writing moves from left to right in lines from top to bottom of page.

### Use of writing
Writes own name.

### Interests and attitudes
Understands that writing is talk written down.

# Writing band C

COMMENT

### What the writer does
Commences writing without assistance. Has a personalized handwriting style that meets most handwriting needs. Checks written work by reading it aloud. Sounds out words as an aid to spelling.

### What the writing shows
Legible writing with recognizable words. Words put together in sentence format. Words written in a logical order to make a sentence that can be read. Upper- and lower-case letters used conventionally. Written sentences that can be understood by an adult.

### Use of writing
Sentences convey message on one topic. Uses 'I' in writing. Writes about feelings, judgment or direct experience. Creates characters from experience and immediate environment.

# Suggested new indicators

VIEWING

LISTENING

SPOKEN LANGUAGE

WRITING

READING

I

H

G

F

E

D

C

B

A

**Writing band** **C**

Now says something in own writing. Is writing own sentences. Is taking an interest in appearance of writing.

## Contexts for observation

**Folders** and **portfolios** of writing in a range of curriculum areas enable teachers to assess the legibility of written work and the degree of control each student has over the conventions of print, including punctuation, grammar and spelling.

**Work samples** will reveal students' ability to control structural features of writing. A work sample also furnishes evidence about construction of sentences, content of writing, handwriting, punctuation, grammatical features and spelling.

Regular **discussion** with students gives an insight into their perception of writing and of themselves as writers. **Parent interviews** will also serve to add to this store of knowledge.

During **writing sessions**, the teacher is able to observe students closely and assess drafting and spelling strategies used. These times are convenient for the teacher to identify students who are confident about tackling writing tasks and to assist those who are not, to confer with every child briefly, and to share students' responses to learning experiences. As a result of observations, notes of significant points can be made.

# Writing band B

COMMENT

### What the writer does
Reproduces words from signs and other sources in immediate environment. Holds pencil/pen using satisfactory grip. Uses preferred hand consistently for writing. Attempts to put 'words' in 'sentence' format. 'Writes' a simple message. Uses sound–symbol linkages. 'Captions' or 'labels' drawings.

### What the writing shows
Use of vocabulary of print (letters, words, question marks, etc.). Use of letters of the alphabet and other conventional symbols. Use of letters in groups to form words. Placing of spaces between groups of 'letters'. Knowledge that writing moves from left to right in lines from top to bottom of page.

### Use of writing
Writes own name.

### Interests and attitudes
Understands that writing is talk written down.

# Writing band C

COMMENT

### What the writer does
Commences writing without assistance. Has a personalized handwriting style that meets most handwriting needs. Checks written work by reading it aloud. Sounds out words as an aid to spelling.

### What the writing shows
Legible writing with recognizable words. Words put together in sentence format. Words written in a logical order to make a sentence that can be read. Upper- and lower-case letters used conventionally. Written sentences that can be understood by an adult.

### Use of writing
Sentences convey message on one topic. Uses 'I' in writing. Writes about feelings, judgment or direct experience. Creates characters from experience and immediate environment.

# Writing band D

COMMENT

### What the writer does
Marks most common words with incorrect spelling when editing writing. Uses ideas, themes and structure from books in writing. Uses concepts of order and time in writing. Reads, rereads and revises own written work. Uses everyday words in appropriate written context.

### What the writing shows
Punctuation used conventionally. Conventional spelling used most of the time; spelling showing recall of visual patterns. Stories that can be read, understood and retold by classmates. Several sentences constructed on one topic in a logical order. A smooth connection of ideas. Beginning, middle and end in narrative writing.

### Use of writing
Writes stories containing characters from outside personal environment. Writes with ease on most matters of personal experience. Writes on a variety of topics. Writes personal anecdotes and letters to friends. Writes for a known audience. Uses a range of written forms — poems, letters, journals, logs, etc.

# Suggested new indicators

VIEWING

LISTENING

SPOKEN LANGUAGE

WRITING

READING

I

H

G

F

E

D

C

B

A

## Contexts for observation

**Writing folders**, in which students list personal achievements, provide insights into individuals' perceptions of themselves as developing writers. The folder also contains evidence of the range and variety of writing being undertaken, and the attempts made to edit, revise and proofread. **Folios** from all curriculum areas need to be examined to gain a more complete picture of each student.

**Work samples** are an important source of information about students, offering the teacher demonstrations of the influences of reading upon writing and each student's capacity to construct longer text that can be understood by peers.

Examination of samples allows the teacher to determine the student's understandings about the structure of text and whether ideas are smoothly connected into a whole piece. Use of punctuation and conventional spelling can also be seen in samples.

**Discussions** with students are a way in which teachers are able to learn how they make decisions about characters, setting, topics and development of their writing.

**Writing circles** provide opportunities for audiences of peers to comment upon and react to writing.

## Writing band C

COMMENT

### What the writer does
Commences writing without assistance. Has a personalized handwriting style that meets most handwriting needs. Checks written work by reading it aloud. Sounds out words as an aid to spelling.

### What the writing shows
Legible writing with recognizable words. Words put together in sentence format. Words written in a logical order to make a sentence that can be read. Upper- and lower-case letters used conventionally. Written sentences that can be understood by an adult.

### Use of writing
Sentences convey message on one topic. Uses 'I' in writing. Writes about feelings, judgment or direct experience. Creates characters from experience and immediate environment.

## Writing band D

COMMENT

### What the writer does
Marks most common words with incorrect spelling when editing writing. Uses ideas, themes and structure from books in writing. Uses concepts of order and time in writing. Reads, rereads and revises own written work. Uses everyday words in appropriate written context.

### What the writing shows
Punctuation used conventionally. Conventional spelling used most of the time; spelling showing recall of visual patterns. Stories that can be read, understood and retold by classmates. Several sentences constructed on one topic in a logical order. A smooth connection of ideas. Beginning, middle and end in narrative writing.

### Use of writing
Writes stories containing characters from outside personal environment. Writes with ease on most matters of personal experience. Writes on a variety of topics. Writes personal anecdotes and letters to friends. Writes for a known audience. Uses a range of written forms — poems, letters, journals, logs, etc.

## Writing band E

COMMENT

### What the writer does
Edits work to a point where others can read it; corrects common spelling errors, punctuation and grammatical errors. Develops ideas into paragraphs. Uses a dictionary, thesaurus or word-checker to extend and check vocabulary for writing. Uses vivid, specific language.

### What the writing shows
Sentences with ideas that flow. Paragraphs with a cohesive structure. Ability to present relationships and to argue or persuade. Messages in expository and argumentative writing identifiable by others, although some information may be omitted. Brief passages written with clear meaning, accuracy of spelling and apt punctuation. Appropriate shifts from first to third person in writing. Consistent use of the correct tense. Appropriate vocabulary for familiar audiences such as peers, younger children or adults, with only occasional inappropriate word choice. Compound sentences, using conjunctions. Variations of letters, print styles or fonts. A print style appropriate to task and a consistent handwriting style.

### Use of writing
Writes a properly sequenced text that has a convincing setting. Creates characters from imagination.

## Suggested new indicators

VIEWING
LISTENING
SPOKEN LANGUAGE
WRITING
READING

A B C D E F G H I

**Writing band E** — Can plan, organize and polish writing. Writes in paragraphs. Vocabulary and grammar are suited to topic. Can write convincing stories.

## Contexts for observation

**Writing circles** provide occasions for teacher and peers to assess cohesion, structure and appropriate use of tense, number and person.

**Written conversation** is another way in which teachers are able to monitor development. Sentence structure, handwriting, appropriate vocabulary and use of standard spelling and punctuation are all easily observed. If written conversations are kept in a separate book for each student and dated, they form part of a record of each student's development over time.

**Publishing** or **presentation** of practical demonstrations or projects requires that students be given time and assistance to work through the necessary conventions. Samples of their 'publications' will provide information, as will **writing folders** and **folios** of work from other areas. Careful consideration of dated work samples will give strong indications of growth in ability to control the conventions of writing.

The **writing folder** is also a source of information about the variety and type of writing being undertaken or attempted. It may contain a list of conventions students believe they have control over, indicating their notions of themselves as writers. Drafts can be compared, and changes noted and discussed.

**Proofreading** tasks can be used to ascertain development in control over grammatical function, punctuation and spelling.

Consideration of a variety of personal and formal **letters** will enable the teacher to learn much about a student's awareness of audience and the demands of context.

Observation of students in **writing** will show use of non-fiction books and papers, plus reference to reading materials, dictionaries, word lists and thesauruses. Significant observations should be noted as part of anecdotal records.

## Writing band D

COMMENT

### What the writer does
Marks most common words with incorrect spelling when editing writing. Uses ideas, themes and structure from books in writing. Uses concepts of order and time in writing. Reads, rereads and revises own written work. Uses everyday words in appropriate written context.

### What the writing shows
Punctuation used conventionally. Conventional spelling used most of the time; spelling showing recall of visual patterns. Stories that can be read, understood and retold by classmates. Several sentences constructed on one topic in a logical order. A smooth connection of ideas. Beginning, middle and end in narrative writing.

### Use of writing
Writes stories containing characters from outside personal environment. Writes with ease on most matters of personal experience. Writes on a variety of topics. Writes personal anecdotes and letters to friends. Writes for a known audience. Uses a range of written forms — poems, letters, journals, logs, etc.

## Writing band E

COMMENT

### What the writer does
Edits work to a point where others can read it; corrects common spelling errors, punctuation and grammatical errors. Develops ideas into paragraphs. Uses a dictionary, thesaurus or word-checker to extend and check vocabulary for writing. Uses vivid, specific language.

### What the writing shows
Sentences with ideas that flow. Paragraphs with a cohesive structure. Ability to present relationships and to argue or persuade. Messages in expository and argumentative writing identifiable by others, although some information may be omitted. Brief passages written with clear meaning, accuracy of spelling and apt punctuation. Appropriate shifts from first to third person in writing. Consistent use of the correct tense. Appropriate vocabulary for familiar audiences such as peers, younger children or adults, with only occasional inappropriate word choice. Compound sentences, using conjunctions. Variations of letters, print styles or fonts. A print style appropriate to task and a consistent handwriting style.

### Use of writing
Writes a properly sequenced text that has a convincing setting. Creates characters from imagination.

## Writing band F

COMMENT

### What the writer does
Writes sentences in different forms: statement, question, command, explanation. Writes paragraphs to develop logical sequence of ideas. Corrects most spelling, punctuation and grammatical errors in editing others' written work. Consults available sources to improve or enhance writing. Joins letters, using linkages where appropriate, to form personal handwriting style.

### What the writing shows
Narratives containing introduction, complication and resolution in a logical order. Longer descriptions and narratives developed coherently. Use of both active and passive voice. A range of vocabulary and grammatical structures. Complex sentences — principal and subordinate clauses. Higher level writing skills in areas of special interest. Understanding of the difference between narrative and other forms of writing.

### Use of writing
Completes standard forms requiring personal information. Makes appropriate use of narrative and other forms of writing.

## Suggested new indicators

VIEWING LISTENING SPOKEN LANGUAGE WRITING READING

A B C D E F G H I

VIEWING

LISTENING

SPOKEN LANGUAGE

WRITING

READING

A B C D E F G H I

## Contexts for observation

**Writing circles** continue to permit students access to a critical audience. The responses offered during these circles are often indications of effectiveness of writing. Form, development of plot and character, structure, tense, complexity of sentences and logical development of writing in narrative and other forms are all areas that can be discussed in this situation. By attending circles, the teacher is able to assess development.

The influence of **non-fiction** material is evident when students write to convince an audience or to illustrate their opinions.

Systematic collection of **work samples** from a variety of sources is important as these are accurate evidence of growth in both content and knowledge of the use of conventions.

'**Publications**', **presented work** from all areas of the curriculum, **folios** and **folders** will all contain information that is significant. In these will be seen each student's handwriting skill, demonstrated understandings of the differences between narrative and other forms of writing, use

of appropriate sentence form, range of vocabulary, and grammatical structures.

Students' beliefs about themselves as writers may be evident in the **writing folder**. Students may record the language conventions they consistently employ or the strategies that they have established. Comparison of work in the folder and listed accomplishments will be a guide to whether students are realistic about their abilities.

Tasks requiring **proofreading** to check grammatical function, punctuation and spelling are windows on the ways individual students approach and solve the audience requirements of standard forms of 'published' pieces.

While students are occupied in **writing**, the teacher is able to move around **discussing** and observing what each is working on. A brief time only need be spent with each student for a wide range of information to be gathered — areas of difficulty, reasons for choice of particular words or phrases, ability to revise and edit text — that can be noted as part of a cumulative record.

# Writing band E

COMMENT

### What the writer does

Edits work to a point where others can read it; corrects common spelling errors, punctuation and grammatical errors. Develops ideas into paragraphs. Uses a dictionary, thesaurus or word-checker to extend and check vocabulary for writing. Uses vivid, specific language.

### What the writing shows

Sentences with ideas that flow. Paragraphs with a cohesive structure. Ability to present relationships and to argue or persuade. Messages in expository and argumentative writing identifiable by others, although some information may be omitted. Brief passages written with clear meaning, accuracy of spelling and apt punctuation. Appropriate shifts from first to third person in writing. Consistent use of the correct tense. Appropriate vocabulary for familiar audiences such as peers, younger children or adults, with only occasional inapp-ropriate word choice. Compound sentences, using conjunctions. Variations of letters, print styles or fonts. A print style appropriate to task and a consistent handwriting style.

### Use of writing

Writes a properly sequenced text that has a convincing setting. Creates characters from imagination.

# Writing band F

COMMENT

### What the writer does

Writes sentences in different forms: statement, question, command, explanation. Writes paragraphs to develop logical sequence of ideas. Corrects most spelling, punctuation and grammatical errors in editing others' written work. Consults available sources to improve or enhance writing. Joins letters, using linkages where appropriate, to form personal handwriting style.

### What the writing shows

Narratives containing introduction, complication and resolution in a logical order. Longer descriptions and narratives developed coherently. Use of both active and passive voice. A range of vocabulary and grammatical structures. Complex sentences — principal and subordinate clauses. Higher level writing skills in areas of special interest. Understanding of the difference between narrative and other forms of writing.

### Use of writing

Completes standard forms requiring personal information. Makes appropriate use of narrative and other forms of writing.

# Writing band G

COMMENT

### What the writer does

Writes in narrative, expository and argumentative styles. Uses a range of writing styles effectively and appropriately for purpose, situation and audience. Uses a range of vocabulary effectively and appropriately for purpose, situation and audience. Edits work to improve the smooth flow of ideas and reorganizes work to make it more readable. Replaces words and sentences during revision of written work. Changes sequence of ideas, adds new ideas during revision.

### What the writing shows

Main and supporting ideas presented clearly. Correct format for letters, invitations. Figurative language, such as simile, for descriptive purposes.

### Use of writing

Shows a range of styles — written conversations, poems, plays, journals. Writes formal and social letters and distinguishes between the purposes of each. Adapts writing to demands of task. Completes complex forms that seek detailed biographical and related information.

# Suggested new indicators

VIEWING

LISTENING

SPOKEN LANGUAGE

WRITING

READING

I

H

G

F

E

D

C

B

A

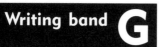

VIEWING

LISTENING

SPOKEN LANGUAGE

WRITING

READING

A B C D E F **G** H I

**Writing band G** Uses rich vocabulary, and writing style depends on topic, purpose, and audience. Writing is lively and colorful. Can do major revision of writing.

## Contexts for observation

Students' recognition of the need to reorganise written work will be seen in the questions writers ask each other during **writing circles**. Main and supporting ideas in writing will also be discussed here.

**Work samples** will show the variety of writing being undertaken, plus the use of correct format for these styles. The different purposes for letter writing — social or formal — will be evident in collected samples of work. Biographical details and related information will be apparent in **anecdotes**, **reflective writing** samples and completion of **survey forms.**

Evidence of editing, from replacing words or sentences to changing a sequence of ideas, will be found by comparing written **drafts** in folios with folders of work from all areas of the curriculum, and in **writing conferences.**

Effectiveness of the writing style and the range of vocabulary used appropriate to the purpose for writing will be demonstrated in the **publication** of written work.

Teacher observation of **writing** and **discussion** with students will discover which students are able to use similes for descriptive purposes.

**Note-taking** activities allow teachers to observe development of skills such as summarizing, recording information and rapid handwriting.

# Writing band F

### What the writer does
Writes sentences in different forms: statement, question, command, explanation. Writes paragraphs to develop logical sequence of ideas. Corrects most spelling, punctuation and grammatical errors in editing others' written work. Consults available sources to improve or enhance writing. Joins letters, using linkages where appropriate, to form personal handwriting style.

### What the writing shows
Narratives containing introduction, complication and resolution in a logical order. Longer descriptions and narratives developed coherently. Use of both active and passive voice. A range of vocabulary and grammatical structures. Complex sentences — principal and subordinate clauses. Higher level writing skills in areas of special interest. Understanding of the difference between narrative and other forms of writing.

### Use of writing
Completes standard forms requiring personal information. Makes appropriate use of narrative and other forms of writing.

COMMENT

# Writing band G

### What the writer does
Writes in narrative, expository and argumentative styles. Uses a range of writing styles effectively and appropriately for purpose, situation and audience. Uses a range of vocabulary effectively and appropriately for purpose, situation and audience. Edits work to improve the smooth flow of ideas and reorganizes work to make it more readable. Replaces words and sentences during revision of written work. Changes sequence of ideas, adds new ideas during revision.

### What the writing shows
Main and supporting ideas presented clearly. Correct format for letters, invitations. Figurative language, such as simile, for descriptive purposes.

### Use of writing
Shows a range of styles — written conversations, poems, plays, journals. Writes formal and social letters and distinguishes between the purposes of each. Adapts writing to demands of task. Completes complex forms that seek detailed biographical and related information.

COMMENT

# Writing band H

### What the writer does
Edits and revises own work to enhance effect of vocabulary, text organization and layout. Edits and revises others' writing, improving presentation and structure without losing meaning or message.

### What the writing shows
Meaning expressed precisely. Organization and layout of written text accurate and appropriate for purpose, situation and audience. Argument, description and narrative presented effectively and appropriately. Vocabulary showing awareness of ambiguities and shades of meaning. Figurative language, such as metaphor, to convey meaning.

### Use of writing
Presents analysis of argument and situation. Sustains organization of ideas, which are justified with detail in extended writing.

COMMENT

# Suggested new indicators

VIEWING  LISTENING  SPOKEN LANGUAGE  WRITING  READING

A B C D E F G H I

**Writing band**  **H**

Is aware of subtleties in language. Develops analytical arguments. Uses precise description in writing. Edits to sharpen meaning.

## Contexts for observation

Students' abilities in editing work to enhance the effect of the writing will be discovered in the **work samples** collected over time. Ambiguity and different shades of meaning may also be observed in these samples, as may figurative language.

**Writing circles**, by their cooperative nature, will show which students are able to edit others' work without losing meaning. From the questions generated and the responses given, these circles will also give information about the appropriateness of the writing.

**Publication** of work, through organisation, layout, and appropriateness of presentation, will be an indication of the purpose of the writing.

**Summarising** books read or **taking notes** from a speaker or during class will demonstrate which students are able to adapt their writing in a manner appropriate to the purpose. Examination of summaries and notes may give additional clues to the writer's interpretations or to intended meanings.

**Documentation** refers to the quoting and referencing that students do in expository writing. It helps teachers to see how well students can justify the points and arguments they make.

# Writing band G

COMMENT

### What the writer does
Writes in narrative, expository and argumentative styles. Uses a range of writing styles effectively and appropriately for purpose, situation and audience. Uses a range of vocabulary effectively and appropriately for purpose, situation and audience. Edits work to improve the smooth flow of ideas and reorganizes work to make it more readable. Replaces words and sentences during revision of written work. Changes sequence of ideas, adds new ideas during revision.

### What the writing shows
Main and supporting ideas presented clearly. Correct format for letters, invitations. Figurative language, such as simile, for descriptive purposes.

### Use of writing
Shows a range of styles — written conversations, poems, plays, journals. Writes formal and social letters and distinguishes between the purposes of each. Adapts writing to demands of task. Completes complex forms that seek detailed biographical and related information.

# Writing band H

COMMENT

### What the writer does
Edits and revises own work to enhance effect of vocabulary, text organization and layout. Edits and revises others' writing, improving presentation and structure without losing meaning or message.

### What the writing shows
Meaning expressed precisely. Organization and layout of written text accurate and appropriate for purpose, situation and audience. Argument, description and narrative presented effectively and appropriately. Vocabulary showing awareness of ambiguities and shades of meaning. Figurative language, such as metaphor, to convey meaning.

### Use of writing
Presents analysis of argument and situation. Sustains organization of ideas, which are justified with detail in extended writing.

# Writing band I

COMMENT

### What the writer does
Writes with ease on most familiar topics in both short passages and extended writing. Uses analogies and symbolism in writing. Uses irony in writing. Uses figures of speech, metaphor and simile to illustrate and support message embedded in extended text. Structures a convincing argument in writing. Can use sustained and elaborated metaphorical language in writing.

### What the writing shows
Extension beyond conventions of standard written English in a skillful and effective way.

### Use of writing
Conveys extended arguments through writing. Adapts to demands of academic writing.

# Suggested new indicators

VIEWING

LISTENING

SPOKEN LANGUAGE

WRITING

READING

I

H

G

F

E

D

C

B

A

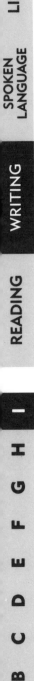
**Writing band** **I**  Writes in many genres. Masters the craft of writing. Is capable of powerful writing.

## Contexts for observation

**Writing circles** are a way of stimulating discussion and provoking thought, which may then be reflected in writing. The subtleties of analogy, symbolism, irony, metaphor and simile can be explored at a writing circle, and examples of these can be read and considered.

**Writing** and **learning folders**, and **folios** of work from all curriculum areas will contain examples of each student's written pieces in response to questions, research topics, debates and formal writing tasks. The appropriate documentation required in academic writing should be apparent in **work samples**.

The systematic collection of **work samples** supplies a significant amount of information about each student and should demonstrate the advanced understanding and use of the skills of writing band I.

School ............................................................... Class ........

Name ................................................................. Term .........

# Writing band H

COMMENT

## What the writer does

Edits and revises own work to enhance effect of vocabulary, text organization and layout. Edits and revises others' writing, improving presentation and structure without losing meaning or message.

## What the writing shows

Meaning expressed precisely. Organization and layout of written text accurate and appropriate for purpose, situation and audience. Argument, description and narrative presented effectively and appropriately. Vocabulary showing awareness of ambiguities and shades of meaning. Figurative language, such as metaphor, to convey meaning.

## Use of writing

Presents analysis of argument and situation. Sustains organization of ideas, which are justified with detail in extended writing.

# Writing band I

COMMENT

## What the writer does

Writes with ease on most familiar topics in both short passages and extended writing. Uses analogies and symbolism in writing. Uses irony in writing. Uses figures of speech, metaphor and simile to illustrate and support message embedded in extended text. Structures a convincing argument in writing. Can use sustained and elaborated metaphorical language in writing.

## What the writing shows

Extension beyond conventions of standard written English in a skillful and effective way.

## Use of writing

Conveys extended arguments through writing. Adapts to demands of academic writing.

# Suggested new indicators

VIEWING

LISTENING

SPOKEN LANGUAGE

WRITING

READING

A B C D E F G H I

# CHAPTER 6
# Spoken language profile records

Spoken language
band **A**

Understands social conventions of spoken language.
Initiates and responds appropriately.

## Contexts for observation

**Talking with and listening to students** during classroom activities provides the teacher with useful information about their understanding and use of oral language, demonstrated by their ideas, confidence, cooperation and responses.

**Dramatic play** in the classroom (dress-up or costume corner) and the playground provides students with opportunities for spontaneous talk, either alone or in role play with others. The teacher may observe students exploring concepts and enjoying language.

**Listening to stories, songs and poems** read and told provides students with opportunities to demonstrate their growing language repertoire and understanding of sounds, rhythm, and vocabulary, and language structures of English in spoken and written form.

Students demonstrate their ability to convey and respond to information in either small or large groups during **share time.**

**Puppet dramatization** of familiar stories provides the teacher with opportunities to observe students' growing confidence and ability to communicate to a large group.

School .......................................................... Class ........

Name ........................................................... Term .........

# Spoken language band A

COMMENT

### Uses of language

Listens attentively to stories, songs and poems. Reacts to stories, songs and poems heard in class (smiles and comments). Joins in familiar songs, poems and chants. Allows others to speak without unnecessary interruption. Waits for appropriate turn to speak. Offers personal opinion in discussion. Speaks fluently to the class. Follows instructions, directions and explanations.

### Features of language

Connects phrases and clauses with 'and', 'and then', 'but'. Speaks at a rate that enables others to follow. Speaks at a volume appropriate to the situation.

# Spoken language band B

COMMENT

### Uses of language

Makes short announcements clearly. Tells personal anecdotes in discussion. Retells a story heard in class, preserving the sequence of events. Accurately conveys a verbal message to another person. Responds with facial expressions. Responds with talk when others initiate conversation. Initiates conversation with peers. Holds conversation with familiar adults. Asks what unfamiliar words mean. Uses talk to clarify ideas or experience.

### Features of language

Reacts to absurd word-substitution. Demonstrates an appreciation of wit. Reacts to unusual features of language such as rhythm, alliteration or onomatopoeia.

# Suggested new indicators

VIEWING

LISTENING

SPOKEN LANGUAGE

WRITING

READING

A B C D E F G H I

**Spoken language band** **B** Experiments and uses language in a variety of ways. Uses talk to clarify ideas and experiences. Body language assists in conveying understanding.

## Contexts for observation

When students engage in **informal talk** (in developmental play activities, such as in the sandpit or in art), teachers gain opportunities to observe them exploring language and interacting socially as they initiate and respond to talk.

Students' experimentation with language during **word play** and the creation of their own rhymes, riddles and songs provide opportunities for teachers to witness their growing vocabulary and concept development, their emotional response to texts and their awareness of the use of language to entertain.

By listening to stories, songs and poems in the **listening area** (listening post, quiet-reading area), students demonstrate their recall of storylines, story and language structures, words and phrases, and share taped stories, songs and poems.

Student responses to literature during **shared book reading activities** (retelling, reading circle,

reading and writing conferences) and **arts activities** (dance, drama, craft) provide information on their growing understanding of stories, characters, plots, settings and language structures.

**Storytelling** in discussion provides teachers with opportunities to observe students' expression of ideas and perspectives relating to personal experiences.

**Reading** and **writing conferences** allow students to demonstrate competence in communicating ideas, clarity in expressing thoughts and ability to request information and accept suggestions.

Students demonstrate their ability to convey and respond to information in either small or large groups during **share time.**

School ................................................................ Class ........

Name ................................................................ Term .........

# Spoken language band A

COMMENT

### Uses of language

Listens attentively to stories, songs and poems. Reacts to stories, songs and poems heard in class (smiles and comments). Joins in familiar songs, poems and chants. Allows others to speak without unnecessary interruption. Waits for appropriate turn to speak. Offers personal opinion in discussion. Speaks fluently to the class. Follows instructions, directions and explanations.

### Features of language

Connects phrases and clauses with 'and', 'and then', 'but'. Speaks at a rate that enables others to follow. Speaks at a volume appropriate to the situation.

# Spoken language band B

COMMENT

### Uses of language

Makes short announcements clearly. Tells personal anecdotes in discussion. Retells a story heard in class, preserving the sequence of events. Accurately conveys a verbal message to another person. Responds with facial expressions. Responds with talk when others initiate conversation. Initiates conversation with peers. Holds conversation with familiar adults. Asks what unfamiliar words mean. Uses talk to clarify ideas or experience.

### Features of language

Reacts to absurd word-substitution. Demonstrates an appreciation of wit. Reacts to unusual features of language such as rhythm, alliteration or onomatopoeia.

# Spoken language band C

COMMENT

### Uses of language

Makes verbal commentary during play or other activities with concrete objects. Speaks confidently in formal situations (assembly, report to class). Explains ideas clearly in discussion. Discusses information heard (e.g. dialogue, news items, report). Based on consideration of what has already been said, offers personal opinions. Asks for repetition, restatement or general explanation to clarify meaning.

### Features of language

Sequences a presentation in logical order. Gives instructions in a concise and understandable manner. Reads aloud with expression, showing awareness of rhythm and tone. Modulates voice for effect. Nods, looks at speaker when others initiate talk.

# Suggested new indicators

VIEWING

LISTENING

SPOKEN LANGUAGE

WRITING

READING

A B C D E F G H I

## Contexts for observation

Students may be observed exploring and learning about language as they **converse informally** in the playground and during practical activities (construction, sand and water activities). Teachers can observe students' increasing confidence and the clarity of their ideas and opinions in discussion.

In **cooperative group activities** students are engaged in the varied purposes of solving problems, exploring ideas, planning and understanding practical tasks. They may be observed as they question, listen, clarify and support the ideas of others.

Students' involvement in **puppet dramatization** of familiar stories demonstrates their growing confidence and ability to communicate to a large group.

Students' **retelling** of familiar stories enables teachers to observe them expressing and exploring their understanding of texts and language with other students.

**Choral reading** can be used to identify students' use of voice to show enjoyment and expression of the rhythm and rhyme of language.

In **cooperative writing**, students demonstrate their ability to communicate and negotiate ideas, clarify meanings and express their thoughts.

During **share time**, students may be observed as they report on and discuss interests, experiences, information or directions relating to something they have created (for example, a model in art or a cake).

When students **provide instructions** to a group on the procedures for playing a game or completing a classroom activity, teachers can observe them presenting information with confidence, using language appropriate to the audience and providing clear and concise information.

## Spoken language band B

COMMENT

### Uses of language

Makes short announcements clearly. Tells personal anecdotes in discussion. Retells a story heard in class, preserving the sequence of events. Accurately conveys a verbal message to another person. Responds with facial expressions. Responds with talk when others initiate conversation. Initiates conversation with peers. Holds conversation with familiar adults. Asks what unfamiliar words mean. Uses talk to clarify ideas or experience.

### Features of language

Reacts to absurd word-substitution. Demonstrates an appreciation of wit. Reacts to unusual features of language such as rhythm, alliteration or onomatopoeia.

## Spoken language band C

COMMENT

### Uses of language

Makes verbal commentary during play or other activities with concrete objects. Speaks confidently in formal situations (assembly, report to class). Explains ideas clearly in discussion. Discusses information heard (e.g. dialogue, news items, report). Based on consideration of what has already been said, offers personal opinions. Asks for repetition, restatement or general explanation to clarify meaning.

### Features of language

Sequences a presentation in logical order. Gives instructions in a concise and understandable manner. Reads aloud with expression, showing awareness of rhythm and tone. Modulates voice for effect. Nods, looks at speaker when others initiate talk.

## Spoken language band D

COMMENT

### Uses of language

Tells personal anecdotes, illustrating in a relevant way the issue being discussed. Recounts a story or repeats a song spontaneously. Retells scenes from a film or drama. Offers predictions about what will come next. Recites poems. Asks questions in conversation. Has a second try at something to make it more precise. Arouses and maintains an audience interest during formal presentations (e.g. report to class, announcement).

### Features of language

Uses a range of vocabulary related to a particular topic. Maintains receptive body stance in conversation. Speaks in a way that conveys feelings (while keeping emotions under control).

## Suggested new indicators

VIEWING

LISTENING

SPOKEN LANGUAGE

WRITING

READING

A B C D E F G H I

Can recount and retell, recite with feeling, and use a range of vocabulary to arouse and maintain audience interest.

## Contexts for observation

The teacher can elicit information about students' oral language development through careful questioning and interaction during **teaching and learning** activities. Students' understanding will be demonstrated during their retelling, prediction and reporting.

After **listening** to or **reading** stories, poems, plays or reports, or **viewing** visual performances, students' retelling provides evidence of their ability to infer, predict, select and organize information, their sense of text forms and their attitudes to language.

**Directed reading-thinking activities** reveal much about students' predictive skills and their use of a range of vocabulary.

While **performing poetry** of different forms, students demonstrate their understanding of mood and imagery, emotional response to text and rhythmic expression.

In **readers' theater**, the teacher is able to observe students' use of voice to convey ideas and feelings, while arousing and maintaining audience interest.

# Spoken language band C

COMMENT

## Uses of language

Makes verbal commentary during play or other activities with concrete objects. Speaks confidently in formal situations (assembly, report to class). Explains ideas clearly in discussion. Discusses information heard (e.g. dialogue, news items, report). Based on consideration of what has already been said, offers personal opinions. Asks for repetition, restatement or general explanation to clarify meaning.

## Features of language

Sequences a presentation in logical order. Gives instructions in a concise and understandable manner. Reads aloud with expression, showing awareness of rhythm and tone. Modulates voice for effect. Nods, looks at speaker when others initiate talk.

# Spoken language band D

COMMENT

## Uses of language

Tells personal anecdotes, illustrating in a relevant way the issue being discussed. Recounts a story or repeats a song spontaneously. Retells scenes from a film or drama. Offers predictions about what will come next. Recites poems. Asks questions in conversation. Has a second try at something to make it more precise. Arouses and maintains an audience interest during formal presentations (e.g. report to class, announcement).

## Features of language

Uses a range of vocabulary related to a particular topic. Maintains receptive body stance in conversation. Speaks in a way that conveys feelings (while keeping emotions under control).

# Spoken language band E

COMMENT

## Uses of language

Presents a point of view to a large audience. Presents materials with consideration for audience needs. Speculates and puts forward a tentative proposition. Uses logic, arguments or appeals to feelings to persuade others. Explores concepts related to concrete materials by describing, narrating or explaining how things work and why things happen. Dramatizes familiar stories, showing understanding. Uses convincing dialogue to role-play short scenes involving familiar situations or emotions. Invites others to participate. Takes initiative in raising new aspects of an issue. Asks questions to elicit more from an individual. Answers questions confidently and clearly in interviews. Asks for the meaning of familiar words used in unfamiliar ways.

## Features of language

Makes links between ideas in discussions. Uses complex connectives in speech, such as 'although', 'in spite of', 'so that'. Uses syntactical structures — principal and subordinate clauses. Uses vocabulary appropriate to audience and purpose. Distinguishes between words of similar meaning.

# Suggested new indicators

VIEWING

LISTENING

SPOKEN LANGUAGE

WRITING

READING

I

H

G

F

E

D

C

B

A

# Uses logic, argument and questioning to clarify ideas and understanding appropriate to audience and purpose.

VIEWING

LISTENING

SPOKEN LANGUAGE

WRITING

READING

## Contexts for observation

**Cooperative group activities** provide the teacher with opportunities to observe students as they take on roles that help communication in the group and the achievement of group goals.

In all areas of the curriculum, groups of students will be observed as they **question**, **discuss** and **debate** issues that arise from their investigations. In presenting their findings to a larger group, students will demonstrate their increased precision and control of the use of language.

During **cooperative cloze activities**, students will be involved in critical exploration of text, language structures and the author's ideas. The teacher may observe them as they speculate, consider the contribution of others and negotiate various points of view.

**Improvisation** provides students with opportunities to demonstrate understanding of character, plot and points of view, and the ability to infer meanings that underlie texts.

**Spoken language profile record**

| School .......................................................... | Class ........ |
| Name ............................................................ | Term ......... |

# Spoken language band D

COMMENT

## Uses of language

Tells personal anecdotes, illustrating in a relevant way the issue being discussed. Recounts a story or repeats a song spontaneously. Retells scenes from a film or drama. Offers predictions about what will come next. Recites poems. Asks questions in conversation. Has a second try at something to make it more precise. Arouses and maintains an audience interest during formal presentations (e.g. report to class, announcement).

## Features of language

Uses a range of vocabulary related to a particular topic. Maintains receptive body stance in conversation. Speaks in a way that conveys feelings (while keeping emotions under control).

# Spoken language band E

COMMENT

## Uses of language

Presents a point of view to a large audience. Presents materials with consideration for audience needs. Speculates and puts forward a tentative proposition. Uses logic, arguments or appeals to feelings to persuade others. Explores concepts related to concrete materials by describing, narrating or explaining how things work and why things happen. Dramatizes familiar stories, showing understanding. Uses convincing dialogue to role-play short scenes involving familiar situations or emotions. Invites others to participate. Takes initiative in raising new aspects of an issue. Asks questions to elicit more from an individual. Answers questions confidently and clearly in interviews. Asks for the meaning of familiar words used in unfamiliar ways.

## Features of language

Makes links between ideas in discussions. Uses complex connectives in speech, such as 'although', 'in spite of', 'so that'. Uses syntactical structures — principal and subordinate clauses. Uses vocabulary appropriate to audience and purpose. Distinguishes between words of similar meaning.

# Spoken language band F

COMMENT

## Uses of language

Asks speaker to clarify ambiguities. Asks questions about words of similar meanings. Elicits information or reaction or opinions from others in conversation. Asks questions to draw information from the group. Indicates disagreement in a constructive manner. Attempts to resolve disagreement or misunderstanding. Supports constructively the statements of others. Attempts to keep discussion on the topic. Makes formal introductions with courtesy and clarity. Tells a story with expression and emphasis, showing confidence, highlighting key points and demonstrating the storyteller's art. Explores abstract ideas (justice, good and evil) by generalizing, hypothesizing or inferring.

## Features of language

Uses a range of idiomatic expressions with confidence. Reacts to an inappropriate choice of words. Makes positive interjections.

# Suggested new indicators

VIEWING

LISTENING

SPOKEN LANGUAGE

WRITING

READING

I H G F E D C B A

**Spoken language band** **F**

Can persuade and influence peers, using language. Clarifies and orders thoughts in conversation. Shows expression of ideas, feelings, opinions and ability to generalize or hypothesize. Speech contains inferences drawn from varied situations.

## Contexts for observation

Engagement in **three-level guide** activities provides students with opportunities to demonstrate their ability to contribute positively to the functioning of the group as they argue, debate and negotiate alternative points of view.

Students' discussion and comparison of their predictions and confirmative evidence in **possible sentences** provide insights into their understanding of vocabulary, a range of issues and text forms.

Students' ability to facilitate group processes will be demonstrated by their active listening and participation in **small-group dioscussion** as they restate, question and clarify information to achieve the group's goal.

Exploration of issues and topics through **critical analysis** of visual and written text provides evidence of students' analysis and synthesis of information.

Students' use of voice, gesture and personality to convey and express feelings, images, mood and experience during **storytelling** is evidence of their command of and confidence in using language, understanding of issues and awareness of audience needs.

Exploration of conflict situations through **role play** provides insights into students' ability to resolve constructively disagreements and misunderstandings.

**Formal introductions** and **responses** to guests and visiting speakers provide students with opportunities to display their confidence in speaking to a large group and their command of language to fulfil social conventions.

School ............................................................. Class ........

Name .............................................................. Term .........

# Spoken language band E

COMMENT

## Uses of language

Presents a point of view to a large audience. Presents materials with consideration for audience needs. Speculates and puts forward a tentative proposition. Uses logic, arguments or appeals to feelings to persuade others. Explores concepts related to concrete materials by describing, narrating or explaining how things work and why things happen. Dramatizes familiar stories, showing understanding. Uses convincing dialogue to role-play short scenes involving familiar situations or emotions. Invites others to participate. Takes initiative in raising new aspects of an issue. Asks questions to elicit more from an individual. Answers questions confidently and clearly in interviews. Asks for the meaning of familiar words used in unfamiliar ways.

## Features of language

Makes links between ideas in discussions. Uses complex connectives in speech, such as 'although', 'in spite of', 'so that'. Uses syntactical structures — principal and subordinate clauses. Uses vocabulary appropriate to audience and purpose. Distinguishes between words of similar meaning.

# Spoken language band F

COMMENT

## Uses of language

Asks speaker to clarify ambiguities. Asks questions about words of similar meanings. Elicits information or reaction or opinions from others in conversation. Asks questions to draw information from the group. Indicates disagreement in a constructive manner. Attempts to resolve disagreement or misunderstanding. Supports constructively the statements of others. Attempts to keep discussion on the topic. Makes formal introductions with courtesy and clarity. Tells a story with expression and emphasis, showing confidence, highlighting key points and demonstrating the storyteller's art. Explores abstract ideas (justice, good and evil) by generalizing, hypothesizing or inferring.

## Features of language

Uses a range of idiomatic expressions with confidence. Reacts to an inappropriate choice of words. Makes positive interjections.

# Spoken language band G

COMMENT

## Uses of language

Asks interview questions that are relevant. Extends another group member's contribution by elaboration or illustration. Helps others to put forward ideas. Summarizes the conclusions reached in a group discussion. Takes initiative in moving discussion to the next stage. Reflects and evaluates discussion (e.g. What have we learned? How did we do it?). Asks speakers for background information. Dramatizes scenes from complex stories, showing understanding of dramatic structure. Role-plays/improvises shaped scenes, showing understanding of dramatic structure. Talks or writes about moral of story heard.

## Features of language

Uses new words spontaneously. Varies tone, pitch, pace of speech to create effect and aid communication. Self-corrects to remove the effects upon audience of a poor choice of words. Comments on some ways in which spoken language differs from written language (e.g. repetitions, colloquialisms, slang, emphasis, incomplete utterances). Talks or writes about special forms of language, such as accents or dialects.

# Suggested new indicators

VIEWING

LISTENING

SPOKEN LANGUAGE

WRITING

READING

A B C D E F G H I

Uses language increasingly to explore ideas, question and summarize discussions. Uses tone to create effect and to aid communication.

## Contexts for observation

Through summarizing, restating, clarifying and elaborating in **cooperative groups**, students demonstrate their positive and active involvement in discussion.

The collection of information from teachers, parents and other students through surveys and **interviews** provides students with opportunities to demonstrate their ability to use a variety of questioning techniques, to select and organize relevant information and to listen and respond appropriately to the ideas of others.

**Critical analysis** of scripted text reveals students' awareness of the particular features of oral and written language.

**Peer** and **cross-age tutoring** provides information about a student's ability to present information clearly using appropriate language, content and supportive listening strategies to encourage a partner's participation.

Rehearsal and interpretation of a scene from a play in **drama workshop** provide the teacher with opportunities to observe students' articulation and defence of interpretation, as well as their organization and expression of ideas through voice and action.

**Improvisation** in role play provides evidence of students' understanding of issues, inference from text, and use of dialogue and gesture to express interpretations and points of view.

School ........................................................ Class ........

Name ........................................................ Term .........

# Spoken language band F

COMMENT

## Uses of language

Asks speaker to clarify ambiguities. Asks questions about words of similar meanings. Elicits information or reaction or opinions from others in conversation. Asks questions to draw information from the group. Indicates disagreement in a constructive manner. Attempts to resolve disagreement or misunderstanding. Supports constructively the statements of others. Attempts to keep discussion on the topic. Makes formal introductions with courtesy and clarity. Tells a story with expression and emphasis, showing confidence, highlighting key points and demonstrating the storyteller's art. Explores abstract ideas (justice, good and evil) by generalizing, hypothesizing or inferring.

## Features of language

Uses a range of idiomatic expressions with confidence. Reacts to an inappropriate choice of words. Makes positive interjections.

# Spoken language band G

COMMENT

## Uses of language

Asks interview questions that are relevant. Extends another group member's contribution by elaboration or illustration. Helps others to put forward ideas. Summarizes the conclusions reached in a group discussion. Takes initiative in moving discussion to the next stage. Reflects and evaluates discussion (e.g. What have we learned? How did we do it?). Asks speakers for background information. Dramatizes scenes from complex stories, showing understanding of dramatic structure. Role-plays/improvises shaped scenes, showing understanding of dramatic structure. Talks or writes about moral of story heard.

## Features of language

Uses new words spontaneously. Varies tone, pitch, pace of speech to create effect and aid communication. Self-corrects to remove the effects upon audience of a poor choice of words. Comments on some ways in which spoken language differs from written language (e.g. repetitions, colloquialisms, slang, emphasis, incomplete utterances). Talks or writes about special forms of language, such as accents or dialects.

# Spoken language band H

COMMENT

## Uses of language

Experiments with and reflects on possible readings and interpretations of a piece of scripted drama. Sustains cogent arguments in formal presentation. Holds conversation with less familiar adults (e.g. guest speaker).

## Features of language

Attempts special forms of language, such as accents or dialects, in own written dialogue. Defines or explains words to cater for audience needs. Comments on bias or point of view in spoken language. Analyzes factors that contribute to the success or otherwise of discussion.

# Suggested new indicators

VIEWING

LISTENING

SPOKEN LANGUAGE

WRITING

READING

I

H

G

F

E

D

C

B

A

Uses and appreciates nuances of language to affect an audience. Monitors and modifies communication to aid understanding.

## Contexts for observation

Active participation in **cooperative group discussion** is demonstrated by students' summarizing of discussion, restatement of group goals, elaboration of the ideas of others and questioning to assist the participation of other group members.

During focused **critical analysis** of visual narratives and reports, students will demonstrate their understanding of varied use of verbal and visual images to persuade or influence an audience.

Students demonstrate personal characterization and interpretation through their use of dialogue, gesture and action in **drama workshop.**

Development of scripts for **dramatization** of an issue or text provides evidence of students' understanding and use of dialogue and dialectic devices to inform, entertain and persuade.

**Formal reports**, **debates** and **expert panel presentations** demonstrate students' abilities to inform or persuade through organizing and presenting issues and ideas to a variety of audiences.

# Spoken language band G

COMMENT

## Uses of language

Asks interview questions that are relevant. Extends another group member's contribution by elaboration or illustration. Helps others to put forward ideas. Summarizes the conclusions reached in a group discussion. Takes initiative in moving discussion to the next stage. Reflects and evaluates discussion (e.g. What have we learned? How did we do it?). Asks speakers for background information. Dramatizes scenes from complex stories, showing understanding of dramatic structure. Role-plays/improvises shaped scenes, showing understanding of dramatic structure. Talks or writes about moral of story heard.

## Features of language

Uses new words spontaneously. Varies tone, pitch, pace of speech to create effect and aid communication. Self-corrects to remove the effects upon audience of a poor choice of words. Comments on some ways in which spoken language differs from written language (e.g. repetitions, colloquialisms, slang, emphasis, incomplete utterances). Talks or writes about special forms of language, such as accents or dialects.

# Spoken language band H

COMMENT

## Uses of language

Experiments with and reflects on possible readings and interpretations of a piece of scripted drama. Sustains cogent arguments in formal presentation. Holds conversation with less familiar adults (e.g. guest speaker).

## Features of language

Attempts special forms of language, such as accents or dialects, in own written dialogue. Defines or explains words to cater for audience needs. Comments on bias or point of view in spoken language. Analyzes factors that contribute to the success or otherwise of discussion.

# Spoken language band I

COMMENT

## Uses of language

Makes effective use of visual or other materials to illustrate ideas. Capitalizes on opportunities offered by responses to interview questions. Asks interview questions designed to elicit extended responses.

## Features of language

Talks or writes about subtle effects of dialogue between characters in film or drama. Uses puns and double meanings. Comments on tone, attitude or emphasis in speech. Talks about quality of speech, such as loudness, pitch, pronunciation, articulation and dialect.

# Suggested new indicators

VIEWING

LISTENING

SPOKEN LANGUAGE

WRITING

READING

I

H

G

F

E

D

C

B

A

Uses language proficiently in its many forms. Is able to evaluate and respond to content and points of view.

## Contexts for observation

When **reporting** on the outcomes of an investigation, students demonstrate their ability to use maps, diagrams, models, extracts and audiovisual aids to help structure and illustrate the information presented.

After watching visual text (theater, film and television), **critical analysis** of elements of the performance allows students to demonstrate their understanding of how these elements contribute to the effect of the performance on an audience.

# Spoken language band H

COMMENT

## Uses of language

Experiments with and reflects on possible readings and interpretations of a piece of scripted drama. Sustains cogent arguments in formal presentation. Holds conversation with less familiar adults (e.g. guest speaker).

## Features of language

Attempts special forms of language, such as accents or dialects, in own written dialogue. Defines or explains words to cater for audience needs. Comments on bias or point of view in spoken language. Analyzes factors that contribute to the success or otherwise of discussion.

# Spoken language band I

COMMENT

## Uses of language

Makes effective use of visual or other materials to illustrate ideas. Capitalizes on opportunities offered by responses to interview questions. Asks interview questions designed to elicit extended responses.

## Features of language

Talks or writes about subtle effects of dialogue between characters in film or drama. Uses puns and double meanings. Comments on tone, attitude or emphasis in speech. Talks about quality of speech, such as loudness, pitch, pronunciation, articulation and dialect.

# Suggested new indicators

VIEWING

LISTENING

SPOKEN LANGUAGE

WRITING

READING

I

H

G

F

E

D

C

B

A

# CHAPTER 7
# Listening profile records

• • • • • • • • • • • • • • • • • • • • • • • • • • • • • • • • • • • • • • • • • • • • • • • • •

The listening profile records have not been developed to the same extent as have those for reading, writing and spoken language. They are presented here in an undeveloped format for trial purposes. The nutshell statements for these profiles are shown below; they illustrate the general thrust of development in listening skills. Band details are presented in the usual style on the following pages, with the exception of bands G, H and I.

**I** • • • • • • • • •   Is a skilled listener, able to distinguish emotive and persuasive rhetoric and to analyze a wide range of spoken genres while listening.

**H** • • • • • • • • •   Distinguishes emotive rhetoric from reasoned argument. Spoken genres are analyzed for meaning and underlying messages.

**G** • • • • • • • • • •   Explores and reflects on ideas while listening; is becoming familiar with a range of spoken forms of language and is able to distinguish between them for purpose, meaning, and appropriate audience.

**F** • • • • • • • • •   Links stories and spoken forms of language to values. Is aware of relevance and irrelevance, pitch intensity, and intonation.

**E** • • • • • • • •   Accepts others' opinions and is developing listening strategies—listening for relationships in stories, poems, etc.

**D** • • • • • • • • •   Distinguishes between social and informational listening; will seek clarification.

**C** • • • • • • • •   Is developing confidence through active listening, responding and clarifying when meaning is not clear.

**B** • • • • • • • • •   Listens for a range of purposes, discriminates sounds in words, and can recall stories told.

**A** • • • • • • • •   Listens attentively, interacts with the speaker and responds with interest.

School ............................................................... Class ........

Name ................................................................. Term .........

# Listening band A

COMMENT

### How the listener attends
Attends to oral stories, poems, etc.

### What the listener does
Recognizes sounds in the environment. Begins to recall detail. Begins to sequence. Follows directions during classroom routines, such as clean-up.

### What the listener demonstrates
Hearing sounds and doing actions simultaneously in action songs. Hearing rhyming words. Using thinking skills in listening activities to sense emotion, predict and sequence.

# Listening band B

COMMENT

### How the listener attends
Listens for a variety of purposes. Listens and sustains attention for increasing periods. Focuses on whole (context) rather than part (detail) when listening to a story.

### What the listener does
Hears initial and final sounds of words.

### What the listener demonstrates
Recall of information from stories, poems, films, etc. Mental pictures while listening to stories, poems, etc. Identification of meaning through speaker's voice (anger, surprise). Thinking skills in listening activities, selecting and giving opinions.

# Suggested new indicators

VIEWING

LISTENING

SPOKEN LANGUAGE

WRITING

READING

I H G F E D C B A

## Listening band A

COMMENT

### How the listener attends
Attends to oral stories, poems, etc.

### What the listener does
Recognizes sounds in the environment. Begins to recall detail. Begins to sequence. Follows directions during classroom routines, such as clean-up.

### What the listener demonstrates
Hearing sounds and doing actions simultaneously in action songs. Hearing rhyming words. Using thinking skills in listening activities to sense emotion, predict and sequence.

## Listening band B

COMMENT

### How the listener attends
Listens for a variety of purposes. Listens and sustains attention for increasing periods. Focuses on whole (context) rather than part (detail) when listening to a story.

### What the listener does
Hears initial and final sounds of words.

### What the listener demonstrates
Recall of information from stories, poems, films, etc. Mental pictures while listening to stories, poems, etc. Identification of meaning through speaker's voice (anger, surprise). Thinking skills in listening activities, selecting and giving opinions.

## Listening band C

COMMENT

### How the listener attends
Listens to others. Begins to show interest in what people have to say. Is aware of non-verbal communication. Is learning to listen critically for main idea and supporting details.

### What the listener does
Hears middle sounds in words.

### What the listener demonstrates
Awareness of the need to be silent, to wait and respond as appropriate. Ability to distinguish between types of speech (a chat, a warning, a joke). Thinking skills in listening activities to plan, compare and begin to make judgments.

## Suggested new indicators

VIEWING

LISTENING

SPOKEN LANGUAGE

WRITING

READING

A B C D E F G H I

School ............................................................. Class ........

Name ............................................................. Term.........

VIEWING

LISTENING

SPOKEN LANGUAGE

WRITING

READING

## Listening band B

COMMENT

### How the listener attends
Listens for a variety of purposes. Listens and sustains attention for increasing periods. Focuses on whole (context) rather than part (detail) when listening to a story.

### What the listener does
Hears initial and final sounds of words.

### What the listener demonstrates
Recall of information from stories, poems, films, etc. Mental pictures while listening to stories, poems, etc. Identification of meaning through speaker's voice (anger, surprise). Thinking skills in listening activities, selecting and giving opinions.

## Listening band C

COMMENT

### How the listener attends
Listens to others. Begins to show interest in what people have to say. Is aware of non-verbal communication. Is teaming to listen critically for main idea and supporting details.

### What the listener does
Hears middle sounds in words.

### What the listener demonstrates
Awareness of the need to be silent, to wait and respond as appropriate. Ability to distinguish between types of speech (a chat, a warning, a joke). Thinking skills in listening activities to plan, compare and begin to make judgments.

## Listening band D

COMMENT

### How the listener attends
Hears the difference between social interactions and information transaction.

### What the listener does
Hears consonants, vowels, blends and digraphs. Hears the difference between hard and soft vowels.

### What the listener demonstrates
Awareness of facts, details, feelings, and values. Ability to listen to and recognize and give an explanation (e.g. in science). Need for repetition or an explanation when meaning is unclear. Thinking skills in listening activities to make judgments, summarize and evaluate.

## Suggested new indicators

A B C D E F G H I

# Listening band C

COMMENT

## How the listener attends

Listens to others. Begins to show interest in what people have to say. Is aware of non-verbal communication. Is teaming to listen critically for main idea and supporting details.

## What the listener does

Hears middle sounds in words.

## What the listener demonstrates

Awareness of the need to be silent, to wait and respond as appropriate. Ability to distinguish between types of speech (a chat, a warning, a joke). Thinking skills in listening activities to plan, compare and begin to make judgments.

# Listening band D

COMMENT

## How the listener attends

Hears the difference between social interactions and information transaction.

## What the listener does

Hears consonants, vowels, blends and digraphs. Hears the difference between hard and soft vowels.

## What the listener demonstrates

Awareness of facts, details, feelings, and values. Ability to listen to and recognize and give an explanation (e.g. in science). Need for repetition or an explanation when meaning is unclear. Thinking skills in listening activities to make judgments, summarize and evaluate.

# Listening band E

COMMENT

## How the listener attends

Is interested in someone else's point of view. Develops strategies for listening to instructions (mental pictures, step by step, etc.). Begins to listen to another person's opinion — to listen for what is important.

## What the listener does

Identifies the sounds of vowels, consonants, digraphs and blends. Uses awareness of sounds to identify consonants, vowels. Uses sounds to identify prefixes, suffices, compounds and syllables.

## What the listener demonstrates

Listening skills to compare and find relationships in stories, poems and conversations. Thinking skills in listening activities, to analyze and hypothesize.

# Suggested new indicators

VIEWING

LISTENING

SPOKEN LANGUAGE

WRITING

READING

I

H

G

F

E

D

C

B

A

Sidebar tabs: VIEWING · LISTENING · SPOKEN LANGUAGE · WRITING · READING · A B C D E F G H I

## Listening band D

COMMENT

### How the listener attends
Hears the difference between social interactions and information transaction.

### What the listener does
Hears consonants, vowels, blends and digraphs. Hears the difference between hard and soft vowels.

### What the listener demonstrates
Awareness of facts, details, feelings, and values. Ability to listen to and recognize and give an explanation (e.g. in science). Need for repetition or an explanation when meaning is unclear. Thinking skills in listening activities to make judgments, summarize and evaluate.

## Listening band E

COMMENT

### How the listener attends
Is interested in someone else's point of view. Develops strategies for listening to instructions (mental pictures, step by step, etc.). Begins to listen to another person's opinion — to listen for what is important.

### What the listener does
Identifies the sounds of vowels, consonants, digraphs and blends. Uses awareness of sounds to identify consonants, vowels. Uses sounds to identify prefixes, suffices, compounds and syllables.

### What the listener demonstrates
Listening skills to compare and find relationships in stories, poems and conversations. Thinking skills in listening activities, to analyze and hypothesize.

## Listening band F

COMMENT

### How the listener attends
Uses values when listening to a story or explanation (animal activities/hunter). Listens for difference between relevance and irrelevance. Listens to pros and cons of argument.

### What the listener does
Distinguishes intensity, pitch, quality and sequence of a variety of sounds.

### What the listener demonstrates
Thinking skills in listening activities, to hypothesize.

## Suggested new indicators

# Listening band E

COMMENT

### How the listener attends
Is interested in someone else's point of view. Develops strategies for listening to instructions (mental pictures, step by step, etc.). Begins to listen to another person's opinion — to listen for what is important.

### What the listener does
Identifies the sounds of vowels, consonants, digraphs and blends. Uses awareness of sounds to identify consonants, vowels. Uses sounds to identify prefixes, suffices, compounds and syllables.

### What the listener demonstrates
Listening skills to compare and find relationships in stories, poems and conversations. Thinking skills in listening activities, to analyze and hypothesize.

# Listening band F

COMMENT

### How the listener attends
Uses values when listening to a story or explanation (animal activities/hunter). Listens for difference between relevance and irrelevance. Listens to pros and cons of argument.

### What the listener does
Distinguishes intensity, pitch, quality and sequence of a variety of sounds.

### What the listener demonstrates
Thinking skills in listening activities, to hypothesize.

VIEWING

LISTENING

SPOKEN LANGUAGE

WRITING

READING

A B C D E F G H I

# CHAPTER 8
# Viewing profile records

• • • • • • • • • • • • • • • • • • • • • • • • • • • • • • • • • • • • • • • • • • • • • • • • • • • • • • • • •

The viewing profile records, like those for listening profiles, have not been developed to the same extent as have those for reading, writing and spoken language. They are presented here in an undeveloped format, for trial purposes. The nutshell statements for these profiles are shown below; they illustrate the general thrust of development in viewing proficiency. The details of the bands are presented in the following pages in the usual style.

**I** • • • • • • • • • • Analyzes and criticizes visual texts for a range of purposes and audiences.

**H** • • • • • • • • • • Considers a variety of interrelationships between texts, contexts, viewers, and makers of visual texts. Constructs meaning from a range of visual texts and justifies this with detailed and well-chosen evidence from the texts.

**G** • • • • • • • • • • Explores different perspectives on complex issues through viewing a range of texts. Considers the context in which texts were constructed, and how the texts reflect them.

**F** • • • • • • • • • • Discusses themes and issues in visual texts, allowing for varying interpretations. Discusses possible reasons for this.

**E** • • • • • • • • • • Selects and uses strategies, appropriate for making meaning, that are appropriate for different texts and viewing purposes.

**D** • • • • • • • • • • Discusses and interprets relationships between ideas, information and events in visual texts designed for special viewing.

**C** • • • • • • • • • • Uses various strategies to interpret visual texts. Enjoys talking about events and characters.

**B** • • • • • • • • • • Enjoys retelling meaning from visual texts with predictive narrative structure. Has favorite characters.

**A** • • • • • • • • • • Recalls events from visual texts with familiar content.

School .......................................................... Class ........

Name .......................................................... Term ........

VIEWING

LISTENING

SPOKEN LANGUAGE

WRITING

READING

## Viewing band A

COMMENT

### Viewing strategies
Focuses on illustration (for details). Recognizes TV program introduction. Tells own story from well-known picture book. Retells own story from favorite TV program.

### Responses
Joins in to accompany speech/song of favorite TV characters. Joins in to accompany speech/song of favorite story characters. Values illustrations as enjoyment. Values television as enjoyment.

### Interests and attitudes
Enjoys a variety of illustrations. Has particular television interests.

## Viewing band B

COMMENT

### Concepts
Is beginning to realize that parts can make a whole

### Strategies
Predicts from visuals; predicts during television program. Is beginning to pay attention to important details. Is beginning to read rebus. Recognizes environmental signs in context.

### Responses
Is beginning to respond to visual information. Is beginning to talk about characters in illustrations. Is beginning to talk about characters on tape.

### Interests
Enjoys talking about favorite illustrations. Enjoys learning about favorite cartoons. Enjoys talking about favorite TV programs. Enjoys computer games.

## Suggested new indicators

I

H

G

F

E

D

C

B

A

School .......................................................... Class ........

Name .......................................................... Term .........

# Viewing band A

COMMENT

### Viewing strategies
Focuses on illustration (for details). Recognizes TV program introduction. Tells own story from well-known picture book. Retells own story from favorite TV program.

### Responses
Joins in to accompany speech/song of favorite TV characters. Joins in to accompany speech/song of favorite story characters. Values illustrations as enjoyment. Values television as enjoyment.

### Interests and attitudes
Enjoys a variety of illustrations. Has particular television interests.

# Viewing band B

COMMENT

### Concepts
Is beginning to realize that parts can make a whole

### Strategies
Predicts from visuals; predicts during television program. Is beginning to pay attention to important details. Is beginning to read rebus. Recognizes environmental signs in context.

### Responses
Is beginning to respond to visual information. Is beginning to talk about characters in illustrations. Is beginning to talk about characters on tape.

### Interests
Enjoys talking about favorite illustrations. Enjoys learning about favorite cartoons. Enjoys talking about favorite TV programs. Enjoys computer games.

# Viewing band C

COMMENT

### Concepts
Uses visuals to follow directions. Is beginning to realize information can be gained.

### Strategies
Uses rebus. Is beginning to project into others' experience.

### Responses
Is beginning to interpret main idea.

### Interests
Recognizes work of a favorite illustrator. Recognizes types of cartoons. Relates why enjoys particular television programs. Is beginning to enjoy Logo.

# Suggested new indicators

VIEWING

LISTENING

SPOKEN LANGUAGE

WRITING

READING

I

H

G

F

E

D

C

B

A

**VIEWING**

**LISTENING**

**SPOKEN LANGUAGE**

**WRITING**

**READING**

## Viewing band B

COMMENT

### Concepts
Is beginning to realize that parts can make a whole

### Strategies
Predicts from visuals; predicts during television program. Is beginning to pay attention to important details. Is beginning to read rebus. Recognizes environmental signs in context.

### Responses
Is beginning to respond to visual information. Is beginning to talk about characters in illustrations. Is beginning to talk about characters on tape.

### Interests
Enjoys talking about favorite illustrations. Enjoys learning about favorite cartoons. Enjoys talking about favorite TV programs. Enjoys computer games.

## Viewing band C

COMMENT

### Concepts
Uses visuals to follow directions. Is beginning to realize information can be gained.

### Strategies
Uses rebus. Is beginning to project into others' experience.

### Responses
Is beginning to interpret main idea.

### Interests
Recognizes work of a favorite illustrator. Recognizes types of cartoons. Relates why enjoys particular television programs. Is beginning to enjoy Logo.

## Viewing band D

COMMENT

### Concepts about visuals
Is beginning to recognize that not everything on screen is true. Knows there is a message in advertisement.

### Strategies
Uses webs to aid comprehension. Uses webs to access prior knowledge. Develops coded messages.

### Responses
Describes TV character(s) vividly. Can interpret main idea. Can describe main idea.

### Interests and attitudes
Has a rationale for favorite TV programs. Is expanding knowledge about cartoons. Is developing recognition of illustrator styles.

## Suggested new indicators

**I H G F E D C B A**

# Viewing band C

COMMENT

### Concepts
Uses visuals to follow directions. Is beginning to realize information can be gained.

### Strategies
Uses rebus. Is beginning to project into others' experience.

### Responses
Is beginning to interpret main idea.

### Interests
Recognizes work of a favorite illustrator. Recognizes types of cartoons. Relates why enjoys particular television programs. Is beginning to enjoy Logo.

# Viewing band D

COMMENT

### Concepts about visuals
Is beginning to recognize that not everything on screen is true. Knows there is a message in advertisement.

### Strategies
Uses webs to aid comprehension. Uses webs to access prior knowledge. Develops coded messages.

### Responses
Describes TV character(s) vividly. Can interpret main idea. Can describe main idea.

### Interests and attitudes
Has a rationale for favorite TV programs. Is expanding knowledge about cartoons. Is developing recognition of illustrator styles.

# Viewing band E

COMMENT

### Concepts about visuals
Is beginning to make references with a variety of visual representations.

### Strategies
Can focus on details but keep whole in mind. Classifies TV programs viewed. States reasons for selecting TV program. Uses a rating scale (school/home devised) and explains why a rating was given. Has rationale for favorite illustrators and artists. Names many forms of visual representation.

### Responses
Relates to people's real contribution. Identifies the 'message' in commercials.

### Interests and attitudes
Is beginning to understand viewer discrimination. Enjoys describing personal opinion of an illustrator's work. Is developing ability to classify video games.

# Suggested new indicators

VIEWING

LISTENING

SPOKEN LANGUAGE

WRITING

READING

I

H

G

F

E

D

C

B

A

## Viewing profile record

School .................................................................... Class ........
Name ...................................................................... Term ........

### Viewing band D

COMMENT

**Concepts about visuals**
Is beginning to recognize that not everything on screen is true. Knows there is a message in advertisement.

**Strategies**
Uses webs to aid comprehension. Uses webs to access prior knowledge. Develops coded messages.

**Responses**
Describes TV character(s) vividly. Can interpret main idea. Can describe main idea.

**Interests and attitudes**
Has a rationale for favorite TV programs. Is expanding knowledge about cartoons. Is developing recognition of illustrator styles.

### Viewing band E

COMMENT

**Concepts about visuals**
Is beginning to make references with a variety of visual representations.

**Strategies**
Can focus on details but keep whole in mind. Classifies TV programs viewed. States reasons for selecting TV program. Uses a rating scale (school/home devised) and explains why a rating was given. Has rationale for favorite illustrators and artists. Names many forms of visual representation.

**Responses**
Relates to people's real contribution. Identifies the 'message' in commercials.

**Interests and attitudes**
Is beginning to understand viewer discrimination. Enjoys describing personal opinion of an illustrator's work. Is developing ability to classify video games.

### Viewing band F

COMMENT

**Concepts about visuals**
Recognizes the difference between TV fact and fiction. Is beginning to understand function of various visual forms.

**Strategies**
Is beginning to understand purposes for different program categories. Is beginning to hypothesize about meaning of visual representation. Applies many forms of visual representation.

**Responses**
Is beginning to relate own opinion to those of a critic. Is realizing and identifying a variety of forms of advertisements.

**Interests and attitudes**
Relates reasons for viewer discrimination. Continues to view and discuss work of a number of illustrators.

## Suggested new indicators

**Viewing profile record**

School ........................................................ Class ........
Name .......................................................... Term ........

# Viewing band E

COMMENT

### Concepts about visuals
Is beginning to make references with a variety of visual representations.

### Strategies
Can focus on details but keep whole in mind. Classifies TV programs viewed. States reasons for selecting TV program. Uses a rating scale (school/home devised) and explains why a rating was given. Has rationale for favorite illustrators and artists. Names many forms of visual representation.

### Responses
Relates to people's real contribution. Identifies the 'message' in commercials.

### Interests and attitudes
Is beginning to understand viewer discrimination. Enjoys describing personal opinion of an illustrator's work. Is developing ability to classify video games.

# Viewing band F

COMMENT

### Concepts about visuals
Recognizes the difference between TV fact and fiction. Is beginning to understand function of various visual forms.

### Strategies
Is beginning to understand purposes for different program categories. Is beginning to hypothesize about meaning of visual representation. Applies many forms of visual representation.

### Responses
Is beginning to relate own opinion to those of a critic. Is realizing and identifying a variety of forms of advertisements.

### Interests and attitudes
Relates reasons for viewer discrimination. Continues to view and discuss work of a number of illustrators.

# Viewing band G

COMMENT

Recognizes scenes that shape the viewer's understanding of a character's role (e.g. identifies scenes that establish a character as a leader). Makes generalizations about the complexities of a character's personality from behavior. Retells a pivotal event and explains its significance to the narrative.

# Suggested new indicators

VIEWING

LISTENING

SPOKEN LANGUAGE

WRITING

READING

I H G F E D C B A

## Viewing band F

COMMENT

### Concepts about visuals
Recognizes the difference between TV fact and fiction. Is beginning to understand function of various visual forms.

### Strategies
Is beginning to understand purposes for different program categories. Is beginning to hypothesize about meaning of visual representation. Applies many forms of visual representation.

### Responses
Is beginning to relate own opinion to those of a critic. Is realizing and identifying a variety of forms of advertisements.

### Interests and attitudes
Relates reasons for viewer discrimination. Continues to view and discuss work of a number of illustrators.

## Viewing band G

COMMENT

Recognizes scenes that shape the viewer's understanding of a character's role (e.g. identifies scenes that establish a character as a leader). Makes generalizations about the complexities of a character's personality from behavior. Retells a pivotal event and explains its significance to the narrative.

## Viewing band H

COMMENT

Understands the interaction between actors' real lives and their constructed film roles (e.g. speculates on the reason for an actor not appearing in a sequel). Empathizes with two characters by inferring from visual clues the nature and context of their relationship (e.g. constructs a dialogue between two characters in a poster). Infers and evaluates the narrative connection between two pieces of viewed text.

## Suggested new indicators

## Viewing band G

COMMENT

Recognizes scenes that shape the viewer's understanding of a character's role (e.g. identifies scenes that establish a character as a leader). Makes generalizations about the complexities of a character's personality from behavior. Retells a pivotal event and explains its significance to the narrative.

## Viewing band H

COMMENT

Understands the interaction between actors' real lives and their constructed film roles (e.g. speculates on the reason for an actor not appearing in a sequel). Empathizes with two characters by inferring from visual clues the nature and context of their relationship (e.g. constructs a dialogue between two characters in a poster). Infers and evaluates the narrative connection between two pieces of viewed text.

## Viewing band I

COMMENT

Understands that authors are sensitive to social concerns when constructing written and reviewed texts (e.g. understands why a girl was added to the book and an Aboriginal girl to the film sequel). Integrates information from related written and viewed sources (e.g. uses information from the film and text extract to explain an inference that a character draws). Interprets and evaluates an image using information from another viewed source (e.g. judges the relationship between a film and a poster of a sequel to the film). Detects and describes complex feelings in a viewed text (e.g. recognizes a character's emotional ambivalence).

## Suggested new indicators

VIEWING

LISTENING

SPOKEN LANGUAGE

WRITING

READING

I H G F E D C B A

## Viewing band H

COMMENT

Understands the interaction between actors' real lives and their constructed film roles (e.g. speculates on the reason for an actor not appearing in a sequel). Empathizes with two characters by inferring from visual clues the nature and context of their relationship (e.g. constructs a dialogue between two characters in a poster). Infers and evaluates the narrative connection between two pieces of viewed text.

## Viewing band I

COMMENT

Understands that authors are sensitive to social concerns when constructing written and reviewed texts (e.g. understands why a girl was added to the book and an Aboriginal girl to the film sequel). Integrates information from related written and viewed sources (e.g. uses information from the film and text extract to explain an inference that a character draws). Interprets and evaluates an image using information from another viewed source (e.g. judges the relationship between a film and a poster of a sequel to the film). Detects and describes complex feelings in a viewed text (e.g. recognizes a character's emotional ambivalence).

## Suggested new indicators

# CHAPTER 9
# Contests — assessment as part of teaching and learning

This chapter focuses on the many contexts that encourage learning about strategies for successful language use. If teachers use supportive contexts in the classroom, students will experience successful language use and learning. Teaching students the strategies involved in *how to learn* means teaching the real strategies of literacy. These strategies emphasise that language is used for learning and developing as well as for communicating what has already been learned.

The use of these contexts assumes that all language users, regardless of age, use similar cognitive processes. Experience rather than developmental stage is held to be the key variable in the evolution of literacy. Learning is seen as continuous. All students will be provided with valuable learning experiences that build on their individual prior knowledge.

In these contexts, students learn strategies that will enable them to solve problems and to use reading, writing, talking, listening and viewing as tools for learning. Although these language modes are seen as objects worthy of study in their own right, the contexts also stress language in use and provide for *learning* language, *learning about* language and *learning through* language as natural components.

The contexts acknowledge the social nature of language and language learning.

Listed below are two possible daily schedules that allow for language-based learning in uninterrupted blocks of language arts time. The schedules themselves are composed of strategies; such components as uninterrupted reading time, reading aloud by the teacher, journal writing and shared writing and reading all demonstrate significant aspects of the reading/writing/listening/speaking/viewing process. The schedules are a guide to what in fact can be a very flexible time that allows the teacher to introduce other strategies at the point of need; for example, the bundling strategy may help students to sort out what they already know and also to understand how paragraphs are organised.

Some useful strategies are then outlined. This is certainly not a comprehensive list, but it is hoped that the strategies described will point teachers towards understanding their value in the teaching–learning–assessment cycle.

## Primary school daily schedule

In a junior school, teachers use daily discussion and sharing, readers' circles, diary writing, story writing and non-fiction writing, and formal writing. Big books are used and revisited, and shared reading takes place. The teacher reads many books from children's literature to the students. This is followed by reader-response discussion, and opportunities for response through art, drama and music.

*Discussion and sharing*  Students group in fours to discuss significant events or to show items of interest. Whole-group sharing may result.

*Journal writing*  Students free-write in journals on self-selected topics. The teacher or another adult may respond to the messages. Special assistance is given here to those in difficulty.

*Story writing*  Students write stories on self-selected topics. Rewrites occur in order to develop finer details and to change spellings. Students are conferenced to encourage extension of the stories, or to develop grammar and punctuation. They may attempt conventional spellings, using a spelling card. The teacher or other adult will respond to the 'closeness' of the spelling and give the student the appropriate word. Spelling cards are not used while students are drafting their writing. The final copy may be typed into a booklet once the student has done all that he or she can. Students illustrate their stories.

*Readers' circles*  Students share, in groups of four, their home-reading books, either before or after they have been taken home. Special assistance occurs here for those experiencing difficulty.

*Formal writing*  Students are taught letter formation.

## Elementary school daily schedule

*Reading and writing workshops* Students develop reading and writing folders or books for their own work. *Writers* draft, edit, revise and proofread their own writing on self-selected or teacher-directed topics, as appropriate. *Readers* self-select their reading material, keep records and gain responses from the teacher and fellow class members as to what and how they are reading .

*Demonstrated writing and shared-book experiences* These are taken regularly.

*Diaries, letters, notes, reports and projects* These are part of the workshop.

*Handwriting* Practice is incorporated into *publication* of work, or may be in the form of individual, group or whole-class lessons as indicated in the diary.

*Spelling* This is learned as part of the language workshop, particularly when the focus is upon proofreading and editing. Individual spelling activities will be included in the diary. Computers and/or typewriters may be used to draft, edit or present written work.

*Portfolios or self-evaluation* Folders will be developed by the students to record work required, points of organisation and comments about what has been learned. Examples of *interest, planning, research, writing* and *presentation* in evaluation of learning projects should be included. The language arts process, which involves *receiving, transforming, expressing* and *appreciating*, must also be considered in self-evaluation where appropriate.

The following examples of teaching contexts may be useful as models from which teachers can develop their own. Such contexts should be planned so that students become aware of learning strategies, which they may then transfer to new situations. These contexts are presented in a much more elaborate form than those given in the preceding chapters. The earlier examples could all be expanded to the same extent.

# Spelling

### Principle

Spelling is learned through being both a writer and a reader. Before publishing, writers must proofread and edit their work to produce standard forms of spelling. Proofreading involves recognizing a misspelling and then doing something about it. This may occur at any time during the writing process, especially with competent writers, but proofreading and producing standard forms of spelling all at once may be difficult for some students.

*Warning* Writers will not become proofreaders if their misspellings are used in ways that result in meaningless and purposeless activities.

### Guidelines

1  Writers underline or circle words recognized to be non-standard, using one or more of the following proofreading strategies.

(a)  Beginning writers who are producing some standard spellings may be asked to underline or circle words that they have 'guessed'.

(b) Older writers may
- stand back from the writing; let the piece rest for a day or two;
- place a ruler under the lines and read forward and backward.
- read backward.

2 Writers produce alternative spellings on scrap paper.

3 Writers disregard any alternatives that are inappropriate.

4 Writers recognize or consult dictionaries or wordbooks for the standard forms.

5 If the writer refers to the teacher, all attempts will be acknowledged, alternative spelling strategies will be discussed or the teacher will assist with the word part that is causing confusion. This discussion could be noted in record keeping.

## Resources

1 A piece of written work, where clarity of meaning has been accomplished and in which spelling is required to be standardized.

2 Dictionaries, word books, familiar books, songs, chants and poems.

3 Teacher, another adult, or another child to act as an authority.

## Learning outcome

Uses a variety of strategies to produce standard spelling.

**Look for:**
- identification of inappropriate spelling;
- referencing;
- use of alternative forms of spelling.

**Record:**
- anecdotal records;
- work samples;
- proofreading of drafted work;
- degree of standard spelling that occurs.

# Home reading

## Principle

By reading with their children, parents are demonstrating that reading is valued. At the same time, it is important that parents understand the reading process so that their children do not receive inconsistent demonstrations.

## Guidelines

1 Students choose their own books from the classroom or other libraries. Appropriate selection of material may have to be discussed with the student. Many students prefer books that have been read aloud.

2 Parents need to know how best to help.
(a) They need to know about the cueing systems used when reading.
(b) They need to talk to their children about what is being read.

(c) They should support and offer positive responses.

(d) They need to give time for students to work out meaning for themselves or to self-correct. 'Try that again' is a useful comment.

(e) If the children are unable to continue, parents should ask a question that directs attention to the meaning before giving words or directions.

### Resources
Access to a stock of familiar, exciting and interesting books.

### Learning outcome
Selects own reading material and shares reading.

### Look for:
- interest outside school hours;
- parent's view of student's reading behavior.

### Record:
- anecdotal notes;
- reading folders.

## Listening post

### Principle
Repeated readings assist students to gain meaning from print where they are able to refine their understandings about written language structures and conventions at their own pace. This strategy is non-threatening and guarantees success; therefore, it is valuable for students who see themselves as non-readers.

### Guidelines
1 Students select a book they wish to hear again.
2 Students follow the print while listening to an audiocassette of the reading.

*One child's response after listening to story*

3 This is repeated as often as the students wish. If a group listen to the same story they can have a readers' circle together, sharing their individual findings.

### Resources
1 Books and audiotapes.
2 Cassette player, listening post and headphones.

### Learning outcome
Shows interest in repeated readings.

### Look for:
- preferences;
- interest and enthusiasm;
- chiming in with stories.

### Record:
- anecdotal records;
- reading logs.

## Readers' circle

### Principle
Interpretation of reading material is heightened by sharing. In readers' circle, readers interact with others to share their unique interpretations of the text.

### Guidelines
1 Readers' circle could involve pairs or small groups.
2 Each reader, in turn, talks about the material he or she has read.
3 Participants ask questions of each other, and read selected passages.

### Resources
Any book, magazine or similar material that has been read. These should be entered in the reading folder.

*Research circles* may be organized when students have read reference material to find information for study. Interpretation of artworks or music can also be heightened using this strategy.

### Learning outcome
Is able to excite others to read.

### Look for:
- response to text expressed through feelings or ideas;
- understanding of print conventions and organization of text;
- developing, integrating and adapting of reading strategies;
- choice of material according to interest, enjoyment and text difficulty;

It is so exciting that I can't wait to read some more. I think the councillor will try to pollute the lake but he dies just when he is going to flip the switch. Yesterday I wondered why if the people went down in the lake how come the councillor would pollute the lake but now I understand that he has to make a choice to save his ppeople. He is very stubborn about knowing the best for ~~this~~ the eople. Something else must hapen because this would not be a good way for the author to solve the problem. She is wery clever at the unexpected and may have the councillor do something I woudn't think about. Mabye Hector will take control and let everyone out in the real world and we know they will be happy there but the councillor doesn't or does he? I don't think ~~Hector will be~~ is strong enough to defey the councillor so the author must have another answer.

- information related to experience;
- understanding of vocabulary and concepts;
- identifying or inferring author's intention;
- evaluation of text on the basis of prior knowledge or experience.

**Record:**
- anecdotal records;
- checklists;
- reading logs.

# Demonstrated writing

## Principle

Learners need to receive many demonstrations of how texts are organized, constructed and used. Students will engage in these demonstrations when the teacher shows how a writer behaves and what a writer does when making meaning in writing.

## Guidelines

1 The teacher demonstrates by thinking aloud and showing how to work from ideas to a draft.
2 This is the teacher's own writing. Editing and revision occur naturally.
3 When drafting is completed, a conference is held.
4 There is no purpose in deliberately making mistakes; enough teaching points will arise as the piece evolves.
5 After completion of the piece, appropriate publishing will occur.

## Resources

1 Overhead projector or large sheets of white paper.

2 Acetate transparencies and fineline markers, Textas.

## Learning outcome

Produces a piece of writing with revision.

## Look for:

- appropriate use of language with consideration for purpose and audience;
- clear and precise instructions;
- confidence in presenting ideas;
- organization and sequence of content.

## Record:

- anecdotal records;
- checklists;
- learning logs.

The Big Chase

Once upon a time a farmer had a good harvest. He stored the corn in the barn. He told the cow that there would be plenty of
A little mouse

THE DOG @ GASD
THE CAT THE CAT GASD
THE MAWS

# Learning logs

## Principle

This recording may assist students to self-evaluate their work and record progress. Writing in this genre will help them to reflect and clarify their views in any curriculum area. Learning logs also allow them to use writing for learning.

## Guidelines

1 Time must be given for students to write before, during and after learning sessions.
2 Logs may be discussed and read if the authors wish.
3 The teacher should also keep a learning log and write at the same time as the students.

## Resource

A notebook appropriately titled for the curriculum area.

## Learning outcome

Is able to reflect upon and write about learning experiences.

> Joshua: Learning Log
>
> I think I am a very good reader and I enjoy it. I have read lots of different books this year but I am now reading a series with 7 books in it. I am good at listening to stories and like talking about them. I realy like drawing pictures about the book becose I get good ones in my mined. I dont like it when the story is just getting good and you have to stop reading. I like reading to myself and I like people reading stories to me becous I can some times get better picturs and becom the charaters or just be in the story.

## Look for:

* evaluation of own reading and literature;
* response expressed through feelings or ideas;
* relation of information to experience or text;
* choice of material according to interest, enjoyment or difficulty;
* expression of point of view;
* identification of relationships;
* exploration of ideas or issues beyond the text;
* identification or inference of author's use of language and intent;
* use of argumentative writing;
* understanding of social comment;
* interpretation of text;
* justification of ideas.

## Record:

* anecdotal records;
* learning logs;
* response journals.

# Bundling

## Principle

To proceed with research or study, the learner needs to be able to predict outcomes. To be able to predict outcomes, prior knowledge has to be connected with the unknown. Some learners need a strategy to accomplish these connections. This strategy may be used to assist in the general studies process.

## Guidelines

1 Write down, on separate cards or sheets of paper, facts already known.
2 Put these cards in order or in sequence.
3 Add more information to each fact.
4 Add more cards where there are gaps in what is known.

Extra information and extra cards become the basis for what needs to be found or discovered.

## Resources

A research topic, cards or paper, pencils or pens.

> All frogs have skin which must be kept moist so that they can breathe through their skin. They also breathe with lungs and through the roof of their mouths. Their nostrils are on top of their heads so that they are able to breathe while their body is under water.

> Many species of frogs are to be found all over the world. In fact there are more than three thousand different kinds. They have been grouped by scientists into different families according to their appearance and where they live. For example, tree frogs have sticky discs on their fingers and toes to help them climb.

> One big difference between the many species of frogs is their different life cycles. Some female frogs lay their jelly coated eggs in air bubbles in water and these eggs develop into tadpoles which grow in the jelly. These tadpoles gradually form limbs and lungs and become frogs. Other frogs lay their eggs in nests in damp ground and these eggs are washed into nearby water to develop. Another species swallows the eggs and the frogs are then born through their mouths

## Learning outcome

Identifies, clarifies and discusses researched information.

### Look for:

- writing adapted appropriately to the purpose;
- interpretation;
- acknowledgement of sources;
- use of significant information.

### Record:

- anecdotal records;
- folios of work.

# Written conversation

### Principle

Written conversation offers a unique opportunity for discovering the written system of language. The focus of this strategy is on successfully conveying meaning. The audience is immediately available to offer response; adjustments are natural to the situation.

### Guidelines

1 Writers work in pairs.
2 Writers ask and answer questions to move the conversation along.
3 Older writers must not speak. If they fail to understand each other, they must indicate this in writing. Beginning writers may read their conversations to each other, if appropriate.
4 The teacher or another adult could act as a writer or responder to draw out a writer's strengths or weaknesses in written language. This is a valuable way of recording progress.
5 Invented spellings should be encouraged, but as writers know that this language event requires more conventional written language, correspondents need to be sensitive to each other.

To MrsoBrin I dot have a sisda but I have a brutta he is e and Hes 4 tis yeuea. Hes name is Andrew My Nana hase a GeGa cat to so has 4 cats.
my cat has a seo pot so at the mint He hast to wok on three legs. from michelle

## Resources

One piece of paper and a pen or pencil for each writing pair.

For recording progress over time, a notebook is more appropriate.

## Learning outcome

Invents spelling so that writing can proceed.

### Look for:

- developing sentence structure;
- use of writing conventions;
- use of a range of vocabulary.

### Record:

- samples of work;
- anecdotal records.

By zena Allen

THE KING'S CAT

Great

I would get the cat down by a mouse or a rat.

# Read and retell

### Principle

Students' understanding of text grows if they are permitted to explore text in a manner related to the way they learned language. This strategy allows them to engage in an activity that uses listening, speaking, reading and writing in ways that resemble the powerful learning processes involved in the learning of language.

### Guidelines

1 Students are immersed in a genre, such as science fiction. The teacher reads to them and

they read sci-fi stories. They talk about what they have been reading. Working in pairs, they list what they have learned about the genre.

2 Students are shown the title of a new story. They predict, in writing, what it might be about, and some of the vocabulary that might be encountered.

3 Working in small groups, the predictions are shared. Each member in turn comments on one other student's predictions.

4 The teacher reads the story. In small groups, students discuss their predictions in relation to the story. They are then encouraged to reread the story as often as they want.

5 When they are ready, they complete a written retelling and proofread it.

6 Working in pairs, they then share and compare the retelling. All contributions are valued.

## Resources
1 Texts to allow immersion in a genre or topic.
2 Multiple copies of a text for retelling.

## Learning outcome
Enjoys literature and is eager to discuss and evaluate it.

## Look for:
- expression of ideas;
- organization and sequencing;
- reproduction of language structures of the text;
- reproduction of ideas and information from the text.

## Record:
- anecdotes;
- learning logs.

# Conclusion

Multiple contexts for assessment are available in every classroom. They provide for many types of observations and rely on many types of validity. By following the methods of action researchers, ethnographers, anthropologists and others who study human behavior in natural settings and seek many types of data, teachers use authentic assessment. In this case the school is taken to be the natural setting for the teaching and learning process. It is possible to describe the method of triangulation as a three-stage process to observing human behavior. The first stage involves identifying the significant features, such as teaching and learning contexts and goals, the second is an intensive observation of practise and the third is a final theoretical study of principles (such as predicted performances in different settings and the psychological constructs and learning development involved.

This approach can be applied to assessment and reporting in schools. Cross-disciplinary triangulation allows similar skills demonstrated in different subject areas to be assessed. Recorder triangulation compares the views of more than one observer. Repeated observation uses the same assessment over many occasions to observe the same behavior. These triangulation methods may be used together to increase the possibility of obtaining a more consistent and more valid assessment that contains sufficient information to suit everybody's needs and purposes.

The teacher is in control of the content and context. Attitudes, interests and other affective characteristics can be assessed. These characteristics need to be given more emphasis in the assessment process in order to reflect their relative importance in the curriculum. The teacher is in control of decisions regarding what competences are valued in the school context, and so must be able to select appropriate assessment procedures.

Triangulation is based on a premise that no one type of measure can adequately describe any phenomenon being studied. A series of related observations, using a different referent for the performance, is likely to provide credible — or valid — information. The teacher can use the literacy profile scales, which encourage the use of multiple methods of observation and which provide criterion-referenced descriptions as part of the authentic assessment process.

**SECTION 3**

# Reporting with profiles

# CHAPTER 10
# Recording and reporting with profiles

## Using the scale to record an assessment

Recording and reporting information about learning has been a difficult issue for many teachers, buildings and districts. There has been a huge amount of research into assessment issues, but very little into reporting and next to none into recording methods. Portfolios have been developed in recent years as a means of storing assessment information, but the communication of assessments has remained unchanged from grade levels, per cent scores or grades. There is little available to give teachers and parents —and others with an interest in student growth and development — about three pieces of information that are important for planning, evaluation and resource allocation.

- What can the students do?
- What rate of progress are they making?
- How do they compare with their peers and with established standards?

The reporting and recording mechanisms developed in concert with the profiles help to answer these questions and to present information to a range of constituencies from students, parents and teachers to administrators, district officials and the general public.

Reporting and recording assessments with the profiles will be illustrated with an example of a student who has been developing in reading and writing a little more slowly than his peers. His name is Gary.

Gary is a Grade 6 boy. He is 14 years old. Obviously, he is older than is usual for his grade level. Progress has not been automatic. Teachers had been encouraging him to write on a range of topics for some years without a great deal of success; then, in fifth grade, his teacher discovered Gary's passion for racing cars and allowed him to read and write and prepare his class talks on this topic without restriction. Gary suddenly became interested in writing, and 'read' as many car magazines as he could lay his hands on; he now willingly seeks out stories and writes on this topic. He was watching the San Marino Grand Prix when Ayrton Senna crashed. His story of the event follows.

## The rating scale

The first method of illustrating and keeping records of an assessment is a rating scale. It is a simple exercise for the teacher to develop overall views of student progress; it is also used for large-scale assessment and survey work when a building or a district or even a state wishes to gather data on a large number of students. Chapter 13 shows this data clearly and discusses the measurement properties of the data and of teacher judgment used to carry out the assessments.

In the first part, a simple rating scale is used to illustrate the application of the profiles in developing a numerical form of reporting and recording the assessment. More on the assessments is presented in chapter 12, dealing with a reading classroom, and then more are illustrated in the section dealing with large-scale assessment.

It is not difficult to assess Gary's writing. It is not usually appropriate to assess from a single piece of writing; normally, we would expect many more pieces to be used and a portfolio of writing samples to form the basis of the assessment. However, in this case we are providing just one piece to illustrate how simple it is to place a student on the scales. Given the background information above and a small amount of writing, (approximately the fifth draft of text), it is possible to gauge Gary's level. In the following example, we can see that Gary has progressively shown indicators of writing development. Starting from band A, the comment section shows how he was rated using the writing profile and a simple rating scale to record the extent to which he exhibited the indicators at each level.

Gary's writing is rated using 3, 2 or 1 for each band level. A 3 means that we believe he is beyond that level, a 2 means that he is developing at that level, a 1 means 'beginning' and a 0 means that we believe that he has not yet reached that level.

It is possible to present different forms of reports that illustrate answers to the following questions.

- Where is Gary now?
- What has his rate of progress been?
- How does he compare with his peers—at the building, the district and other levels in the system (norms)?

---

# Writing band A

### What the writer does
Uses writing implement to make marks on paper. Explains the meaning of marks (word, sentence, writing, letter). Copies 'words' from signs in immediate environment. 'Reads', understands and explains own 'writing'.

### What the writing shows
Understanding of the difference between picture and print. Use of some recognizable symbols in writing.

### Use of writing
Comments on signs and other symbols in immediate environment. Uses a mixture of drawings and 'writing' to convey and support an idea.

COMMENT    3

- Gary certainly makes marks, copies words from the environment, even the newspaper.
- We can conclude that Gary is beyond band A.

· · · · · · · · · · · · · · · · · · · · · · · · · · · · · · · · · · · · · · · · · · · · · · · · · · · ·

# Writing band B

### What the writer does
Reproduces words from signs and other sources in immediate environment. Holds pencil/pen using satisfactory grip. Uses preferred hand consistently for writing. Attempts to put 'words' in 'sentence' format. 'Writes' a simple message. Uses sound–symbol linkages. 'Captions' or 'labels' drawings.

### What the writing shows
Use of vocabulary of print (letters, words, question marks, etc.). Use of letters of the alphabet and other conventional symbols. Use of letters in groups to form words. Placing of spaces between groups of 'letters'. Knowledge that writing moves from left to right in lines from top to bottom of page.

### Use of writing
Writes own name.

### Interests and attitudes
Understands that writing is talk written down.

COMMENT    3

- He is reproducing words from the newspaper and other media.
- He uses all of these conventions.
- Words, spaces, directionality.
- Signs his name at the end of the work.

· · · · · · · · · · · · · · · · · · · · · · · · · · · · · · · · · · · · · · · · · · · · · · · · · · · ·

# Writing band C

## What the writer does

Commences writing without assistance. Has a personalized handwriting style that meets most handwriting needs. Checks written work by reading it aloud. Sounds out words as an aid to spelling.

## What the writing shows

Legible writing with recognizable words. Words put together in sentence format. Words written in a logical order to make a sentence that can be read. Upper- and lower-case letters used conventionally. Written sentences that can be understood by an adult.

## Use of writing

Sentences convey message on one topic. Uses 'I' in writing. Writes about feelings, judgment or direct experience. Creates characters from experience and immediate environment.

COMMENT
- Gary will write on racing cars without prompting, uses sentences and has paragraph structure.
- Writing is legible, upper and lower case are used and the text can be read by an adult.
- He writes in the first person, expresses feelings and creates characters from his environment.

• • • • • • • • • • • • • • • • • • • • • • • • • • • • • • • • • • • • • • • • • • • • • • • •

# Writing band D

COMMENT    2

## What the writer does

Marks most common words with incorrect spelling when editing writing. Uses ideas, themes and structure from books in writing. Uses concepts of order and time in writing. Reads, rereads and revises own written work. Uses everyday words in appropriate written context.

## What the writing shows

Punctuation used conventionally. Conventional spelling used most of the time; spelling showing recall of visual patterns. Stories that can be read, understood and retold by classmates. Several sentences constructed on one topic in a logical order. A smooth connection of ideas. Beginning, middle and end in narrative writing.

## Use of writing

Writes stories containing characters from outside personal environment. Writes with ease on most matters of personal experience. Writes on a variety of topics. Writes personal anecdotes and letters to friends. Writes for a known audience. Uses a range of written forms — poems, letters, journals, logs, etc.

COMMENT
- Can edit his work, (this is the fifth version of his text), revises writing.
- Punctuation is not used conventionally, story could be read by classmates with difficulty.
- Sentences vary in logical sequence, order of ideas is established.
- Does not write on a range of topics, but is restricted.
- In most aspects Gary has not yet moved beyond band D.

• • • • • • • • • • • • • • • • • • • • • • • • • • • • • • • • • • • • • • • • • • • • • • • •

# Writing band E

COMMENT    1

## What the writer does

Edits work to a point where others can read it; corrects common spelling errors, punctuation and grammatical errors. Develops ideas into paragraphs. Uses a dictionary, thesaurus or word-checker to extend and check vocabulary for writing. Uses vivid, specific language.

## What the writing shows

Sentences with ideas that flow. Paragraphs with a cohesive structure. Ability to present relationships and to argue or persuade. Messages in expository and argumentative writing identifiable by others, although some information may be omitted. Brief passages written with clear meaning, accuracy of spelling and apt punctuation. Appropriate shifts from first to third person in writing. Consistent use of the correct tense. Appropriate vocabulary for familiar audiences such as peers, younger children or adults, with only occasional inappropriate word choice. Compound sentences, using conjunctions. Variations of letters, print styles or fonts. A print style appropriate to task and consistent handwriting style.

## Use of writing

Writes a properly sequenced text that has a convincing setting. Creates characters from imagination.

COMMENT
- Common spelling errors are not all corrected, the writing still contains punctuation and grammatical errors.
- Gary is only showing very early signs of band E behavior if any at all.

# The literacy rocket

It is possible to develop a graphic representation of a student's progress using the nutshell statements and a graph illustrating the full range of the continuum. If the range where a student group is expected to be developing is located on the graph (from the descriptive data in chapter 13) and the teacher then adds each student's approximate level

# Writing band F

### What the writer does

Writes sentences in different forms: statement, question, command, explanation. Writes paragraphs to develop logical sequence of ideas. Corrects most spelling, punctuation and grammatical errors in editing others' written work. Consults available sources to improve or enhance writing. Joins letters, using linkages where appropriate, to form personal handwriting style.

### What the writing shows

Narratives containing introduction, complication and resolution in a logical order. Longer descriptions and narratives developed coherently. Use of both active and passive voice. A range of vocabulary and grammatical structures. Complex sentences — principal and subordinate clauses. Higher level writing skills in areas of special interest. Understanding of the difference between narrative and other forms of writing.

### Use of writing

Completes standard forms requiring personal information. Makes appropriate use of narrative and other forms of writing.

- Lacks capacity to write in different forms.
- Coherence of narrative depends on a sympathetic reader.
- Lacks complex sentences.
- Shows no understanding of different forms of writing in this piece.
- Gary has not yet reached band F.

# Writing band G

### What the writer does

Writes in narrative, expository and argumentative styles. Uses a range of writing styles effectively and appropriately for purpose, situation and audience. Uses a range of vocabulary effectively and appropriately for purpose, situation and audience. Edits work to improve the smooth flow of ideas and reorganizes work to make it more readable. Replaces words and sentences during revision of written work. Changes sequence of ideas, adds new ideas during revision.

### What the writing shows

Main and supporting ideas presented clearly. Correct format for letters, invitations. Figurative language, such as simile, for descriptive purposes.

### Use of writing

Shows a range of styles — written conversations, poems, plays, journals. Writes formal and social letters and distinguishes between the purposes of each. Adapts writing to demands of task. Completes complex forms that seek detailed biographical and related information.

of development, a very rich contextualised description of student performance becomes available. This is illustrated in Figure 10.1, which we call the *literacy rocket*. There are several components to the rocket. First, the nutshell statements illustrate the progression of literacy described by the profiles. Second, the box in the stem of the rocket presents the expected level for the middle 50 per cent of a year-level cohort. Finally, the rocket presents the teacher with an opportunity to place a student on the profile scale using both normative and criterion-referenced information. Note that since the nutshell statements can be translated into several languages, parents who do not speak English can be *shown in graphic* form, their child's progress in literacy.

This is such a simple task. Suppose that Gary's work were contained in a portfolio with reading logs, tapes of his speaking, reports of his discussions and so on; the teacher would only need to build the profile once every few weeks. The richness of the assessment would feed into

teaching and be based directly on the assessment of the student's work. The teacher only has to mark the rocket as illustrated with a small shaded region to show Gary's progress; now Gary and his parents can be shown what he has achieved, where he is heading, and how he compares with others in Grade 6. We have here both norm-referenced interpretation and criterion-referenced interpretation on the same report. Blackline masters of the rocket are provided in appendix 3 for all profile scales.

## Recording rate of progress

Another form of individual record keeping and reporting was devised by a school district in New York State; they adapted box plots and whisker plots and made them fit their own school. Box and whisker plots (illustrated in chapter 13) are a graphic way of presenting the distribution of student performance; they present the standards of the school (or any other descriptive data) and allow the student growth to be monitored from

# Writing Profile Rocket

Class .......... 6 ..........................  School ...*Central Elementary*...

Teacher ....*Ms Smith*................  Student ...*Gary Black*...........

Is aware of subtleties in language. Develops analytical arguments. Uses precise description in writing. Edits to sharpen meaning.

**I** · · · · · · · Writes in many genres. Masters the craft of writing. Is capable of powerful writing.

**H**

**G** · · · · · · · Uses rich vocabulary, and writing style depends on topic, purpose and audience. Writing is also lively and colorful. Can do major revisions of writing.

Can describe things well. Can skillfully write and tell a story or describe phenomena. Now has skills to improve writing.

**F**

**E** · · · · · · · Can plan, organize and polish writing. Writes in paragraphs. Voaculary and grammar are suited to topic. Can write convincing stories.

Can write own stories. Changes words and spelling until satisfied with the result.

**D**

**C** · · · · · · · Now says something in own writing. Is writing own sentences. Is taking interest in appearence of writing.

Is learning about handwriting. Knows what letters and words are and can talk about ideas in own writing. Is starting to write recognizable letters and words.

**B**

**A** · · · · · · · Knows that writing says something. Is curious about environmental print. Is starting to see patterns.

50% of the Grade 6 students can be located within this range. Norms for all grades can be identified by locating the 'box' from the box and whisker plot in Chapter 13 for the relevant skill.

Gary is estimated to be at about this location on the profile. See the worked example for writing shown on pages 106-8.

*Figure 10.1*

year to year and compared with those data. The report is accompanied with the full text of the profiles. Obviously, the use of criterion-referenced reporting and recording formats allows great flexibility and enormous communication ability on the part of the teacher and the school. Gary's progress can now be plotted over a number of years; the teacher can plot his level on the profiles at the same time each year, perhaps in the spring, and illustrate how he has grown and developed. The norm (box) for the grade level can be used as a reference point and used to illustrate the rate of progress. In Gary's case, there has been dramatic growth in both reading and writing from Grade 5 to Grade 6; if this information is supplemented with portfolio examples of his work, parents and teachers alike can gain a very clear understanding of his development. This is illustrated in Figure 10.2, in which his level is represented by the dot (•) under the box plots. His progress over the six years of school is represented by his position in the spring term each year, when his achievement with regard to reading, writing and spoken language on the profiles has been plotted and the information added to his portfolio.

The permanent record of Gary's language arts development shows some remarkable development in the upper elementary years. Teachers would see that Gary has had a slow beginning and the teacher who recorded such a dramatic jump in development would almost certainly be asked what had happened. What was the evidence for such a change? This clearly overcomes an important difficulty in assessment programs — labelling; students can often be labelled as underachievers and given little encouragement of improvement. Gary's teacher, however, can show that improvement is occurring, and so the potential for Gary to be labelled as a permanent underachiever is diminished. Moreover, because it is a decision and a judgment made on the basis of continuous information and observation in class, there is little chance of the change being dismissed as an aberration attributable to a different testing program or to coaching for a testing program. The profiles can, as in the case of Gary, help to overcome many of the negative aspects of assessment.

In this case, the teachers in the school collected the data and developed the school's own box and whisker plots for the report. It is also possible to use norms from the research studies on profiles. For this reason, blackline masters based on average expected rates of progress — as demonstrated by a sample of over 2000 students — have been presented in the appendix for school use. Schools could perhaps develop their own norms over a number of years and use a stab set of box plots; in the meantime, it is suggested that the plots presented in the appendix are used.

## The class record

Using a standard class list, the profiles can be mapped onto the list using the nutshell statements to illustrate levels of growth. This helps to establish local comparisons and to give the teacher a continuous overview of the relative development of all students in the class.

The class record forms included in appendix 3 can be copied and covered with a laminating sheet or with plastic so that a water-based felt pen can be used to show growth, adding a different color each term. A thermometer approach (that is, adding small bits to the record as improvement is seen and matched to the bands) would be best in this case so that the development and accumulation of skills can be seen. Examples of Gary's class are illustrated in Figure 10.3. It can be seen that some students have made more progress than others, but Gary's progress is shown to be spectacular and recent.

In this example it can be seen that although Gary is below the expected range for his grade level, there are other students in the class who are at similar levels. The range in the class is quite large and the teacher needs to develop an instructional approach to compensate for the range of development; this alone illustrates to teachers and others that one approach alone can never work successfully. Graphic reports may be supplemented with descriptive reports, but generally teachers will not have time to write long descriptive reports about student development; instead, profiles provide the opportunity to use the indicators to frame descriptive reports that show what the students have completed, what they are working on now and the next signs of progress that can be expected. Parents also can be involved in helping to develop those signs by working with the students. The descriptive report on page 113 describes Gary's progress; this style of report might be best accompanied by the box plot style overview or by the rocket chart in order to put the report into context.

# Central School District

It is important to note that the reading and writing bands do not interrelate; therefore, no comparison can be made between the two.

Student ...... *Gary* ......

## Reading band continuum

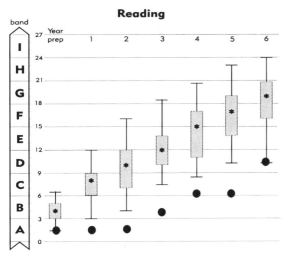

## Writing band continuum

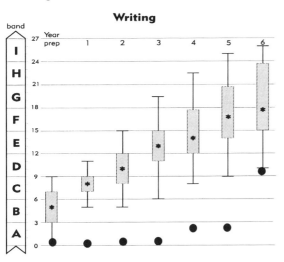

## Spoken language band continuum

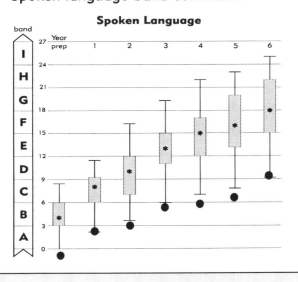

*Figure 10.2*

# Writing Profile Class Record

Class .......... 6 .......... School .. *Tanda Central* ..............

Teacher .......... *P. Smith* ..............

| Band | | Gary | Peter | Simon | Matthew | Max | Amanda | Sally | Sue Ann | Anne | Lois | Patricia | Sylvia | Marie | Abdul | Kerrie | Patty | Richard | Adele | Mandy | |
|---|---|---|---|---|---|---|---|---|---|---|---|---|---|---|---|---|---|---|---|---|---|
| **I** | Writes in many genres. Masters the craft of writing. Is capable of powerful writing. | | | | | | | | | | | | | | | | | | | | |
| **H** | Is aware of subtleties in language. Develops analytical arguments. Uses precise description in writing. Edits to sharpen meaning. | | | | | | | | | | | | | | | | | | | | |
| **G** | Uses rich vocabulary, and writing style depends on topic, purpose and audience. Writing is also lively and colorful. Can do major revisions of writing. | | | | | | | | | | | | | | | | | | | | |
| **F** | Can describe things well. Can skillfully write and tell a story or describe phenomena. Now has skills to improve writing. | | | | | | | | | | | | | | | | | | | | |
| **E** | Can plan, organize and polish writing. Writes in paragraphs. Vocabulary and grammar are suited to topic. Can write convincing stories. | | | | | | | | | | | | | | | | | | | | |
| **D** | Can write own stories. Changes words and spelling until satisfied with the result. | | | | | | | | | | | | | | | | | | | | |
| **C** | Now says something in own writing. Is writing own sentences. Is taking interest in appearence of writing. | | | | | | | | | | | | | | | | | | | | |
| **B** | Is learning about handwriting. Knows what letters and words are and can talk about ideas in own writing. Is starting to write recognizable letters and words. | | | | | | | | | | | | | | | | | | | | |
| **A** | Knows that writing says something. Is curious about environmental print. Is starting to see patterns. | | | | | | | | | | | | | | | | | | | | |

*Figure 10.3*

Gary is reading a wider range of materials now. He is able to identify appropriate reading materials for his interests and tends to read a lot of materials on racing cars if the materials are well illustrated and the captions are simple. He is prepared to tackle some materials on cars even when the text is difficult. This is particularly true if there are many pictures to help with the reading. He will need to broaden his reading materials in the next year. He seeks out classmates and others in the school to discuss the materials he reads.

His written work also reflects the books he reads. He writes his own stories and can check his spelling to a limited degree. His grammar will soon improve as he learns more about sentences and paragraphs and as he reads a wider range of materials. He writes about the things he has seen on TV and in the newspapers about car racing. The writing also reflects the conversations he holds with his classmates and others at school. His range of topics is limited but recently he has begun to write letters and other forms of writing. He can be expected to improve in both range and content of writing in the near future as he begins to develop ways of planning his writing and his command of grammar and spelling.

# CHAPTER 11
# Profiling the literacy skills of students with special needs

● ● ● ● ● ● ● ● ● ● ● ● ● ● ● ● ● ● ● ● ● ● ● ● ● ● ● ● ● ● ● ● ● ● ● ● ● ● ● ● ● ● ● ● ● ● ● ●

The assessment of language competency and growth has been a major stumbling block in the educational delivery system developed in the United States for 'special education'. To begin with, the assumption that group-administered classroom tests of reading, spelling, writing mechanics, and so on were inappropriate for assessing the capabilities of children being evaluated for special education placement led to the development of individually administered tests given only to such children. These tests were often developed by clinicians who were unfamiliar with classroom curriculum or instructional practise. Furthermore, the scores obtained from administering such instruments were interpreted in ways that made sense to clinicians, but not to either classroom teachers or parents. Although the tests had names such as 'reading comprehension', the results could not be related to those of other students in the classroom, which only increased the pressure to deal with those 'special' students somewhere outside the 'regular' classroom.

For children who are identified as requiring special education but who are 'mainstreamed' in the regular classroom, the questions relative to their inclusion in district-wide testing programs have raised further roadblocks. The same realization that the traditional multiple-choice, timed, norm-referenced tests were not as valid for identified students as they might be for others led to the inclusion in individual educational plans (IEPs) of testing modifications. In order to make the tests more valid for those children, they were to be given in quiet places, free from distractions (that is, out of the classroom) given without time limits and dictated to the children, so that reading demands were negated. Unfortunately, such modifications of the traditional tests make the interpretation of the scores invalid all over again.

The problems inherent in the use of 'test modifications' have been recognized, and in many places mainstreamed students have been excused from district-wide testing altogether; additionally, identified students in self-contained classrooms have routinely been excused from this type of testing. Thus, albeit for well-intentioned reasons, students who are classified as requiring special educational programs have been unable to demonstrate the degree to which they are able to perform the literacy tasks their counterparts in the regular classroom perform. Therefore, as well, parents, staff, and school-board members have been unable to evaluate the degree to which the special education program has enabled those children to learn the same curriculum, despite their handicapping conditions.

Taken together, the circumstances described above have led to the widening separation of 'special ed' and 'regular ed', with students unable to move from one program to the other as might be desirable, teachers unable to talk to one another about cognitive performance of special-needs students, and parents perplexed about 'what the scores mean' and whether students are growing as they should or could. What has been needed — and what is now provided by *Literacy Profiles* — is a way of talking about literacy development that is equally valid for all students, a method that is independent of differentiated curriculum and instructional methods, a mechanism capable of capturing and reporting even small increments of growth, and one with results expressed in language that can be understood by all the stakeholders.

What are the characteristics that enable *Literacy Profiles* to make the move from 'regular ed' to 'special ed' without missing a beat?

1 The pointers or attributes on the bands are observable behaviors — 'outcomes', if you will — that are not specific to any curriculum or instructional method. Thus, the profiles are not curriculum-bound, nor do they mimic any particular method of teaching. How a student acquired a behavior is, in this sense, irrelevant.

2 Interpretation is not either age- or grade-based. Any person, child or adult, developmentally delayed, handicapped or otherwise, may be observed and profiled on the bands. In this respect, the profiles are criterion-referenced.

3 The language used in the profiles is 'plain English' rather than technical terminology or

'educationese'. Parents and school personnel can be assured that they are on the same wavelength in their discussion of an individual's profile.

4  Because performance is described as a band of behaviors rather than as a point, idiosyncratic patterns of development can be noted and acknowledged while the overall profile of the individual is also apparent and may be compared with those of others, whether identified or not.

5  Since each band includes numerous pointer statements, relatively small increments of growth or change — even within a single band — may be documented. In other words, the profiles are extremely sensitive to change or growth or, on the other hand, to lack of growth in important behaviors.

6  Likewise, the abundance of pointer statements for each band ensures that if any should be inappropriate to a given individual because of the handicapping condition, they may be ignored without doing violence to the scale underlying the profiles.

7  The richness of pointers for each band and the fact that all individuals develop across several bands at the same time make the completed profile ideally suited to the task of developing a new IEP. The design of the profiles helps in the identification of both which pointers to look for (and teach to) next and the contexts in which they might be taught and/or observed.

8  Because the performance of identified individuals is described in the same way as that of all the other children, the profiles may be used to clarify the degree to which a child may be 'mainstream', as well as the ways in which classroom instruction may need to be modified for that individual. Likewise the 'coping skills' an individual needs to develop in order to be successful in the mainstream classroom may be more easily identified.

To this point, the discussion has emphasized the advantages the profiles provide to parents and the school administration, with only passing reference to the very positive influences they may have on the identified individuals themselves. The emphasis in profiling is on what the student has demonstrated ability to do, rather than on what has not yet been learned. A student's own progress, rather than its relationship to grade (or age) norms or standards, is what is emphasized. Thus, successes, even small ones, can be documented and reported — an extremely reinforcing experience for students who have too often been evaluated in terms of their shortcomings rather than their strengths. The profiles also make it easier to see the direction in which changes are headed and what next evidences of growth should be anticipated. The student may well be able to share in this planning of next steps and the observation of progress, taking pride of ownership for growth, as well.

Two examples of writing profiles are given below.

**Darren**

Samples of Darren's writing are shown below the teacher's ratings on his reading.

Darren has just turned nine. His early years in school were quite unproductive owing to emotional problems. He is labelled 'emotionally disturbed' and is in a self-contained classroom within his local school. In the one year since that

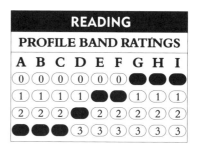

| READING | | | | | | | | |
|---|---|---|---|---|---|---|---|---|
| **PROFILE BAND RATINGS** | | | | | | | | |
| A | B | C | D | E | F | G | H | I |

SEAt21\993

I am going to mainstreaming in math.

4|6|94
I want to be a basketball player. I want to be on the Chicago Bulls. I would like to be just like Michael Jordan. Michael Jordan is the best dunker in the world. I would have to prictes. If I was a basketball player I would

placement, his reading level has improved by two grade levels and his written language has been sparked by his awareness of the world and his belief in himself. He is interested in lots of topics — sports, science and music — so his selection of books shows great variety. He loves to publish his own works and he learns to read those of the other students. He is well on his way to success in school and soon he will be able to shed his 'label' and return to the mainstream classroom.

In Darren's writing profile record, the shading indicates sections highlighted by the teacher.

# Writing Profile Rocket

Class ..................................................... School ..........................................
Teacher ................................................. Student .......... *Darren* ..................

**I** • • • • • • Writes in many genres. Masters the craft of writing. Is capable of powerful writing.

Is aware of subtleties in language. Develops analytical arguments. Uses precise description in writing. Edits to sharpen meaning. • • • • • • **H**

**G** • • • • • • Uses rich vocabulary, and writing style depends on topic, purpose and audience. Writing is also lively and colorful. Can do major revisions of writing.

Can describe things well. Can skillfully write and tell a story or describe phenomena. Now has skills to improve writing. • • • • • • **F**

**E** • • • • • • Can plan, organize and polish writing. Writes in paragraphs. Voaculary and grammar are suited to topic. Can write convincing stories.

Can write own stories. Changes words and spelling until satisfied with the result. • • • • • • **D**

**C** • • • • • • Now says something in own writing. Is writing own sentences. Is taking interest in appearence of writing.

Is learning about handwriting. Knows what letters and words are and can talk about ideas in own writing. Is starting to write recognizable letters and words. • • • • • • **B**

**A** • • • • • • Knows that writing says something. Is curious about environmental print. Is starting to see patterns.

[shaded box] 50% of the Grade ☐ students can be located within this range. Norms for all grades can be identified by locating the 'box' from the box and whisker plot in Chapter 13 for the relevant skill.

[black box] The student is estimated to be at about this location on the profile. See the worked example for writing shown on pages 106-8.

*Figure 11.1*

# Writing Profile Record

Class ................................................ School .............................................

Name .......... *Darren* ..................................... Term ...............................................

## Writing band C

**What the writer does**

Commences writing without assistance. Has a personalized handwriting style that meets most handwriting needs. Checks written work by reading it aloud. Sounds out words as an aid to spelling.

**What the writing shows**

Legible writing with recognizable words. Words put together in sentence format. Words written in a logical order to make a sentence that can be read. Upper- and lower-case letters used conventionally. Written sentences that can be understood by an adult.

**Use of writing**

Sentences convey message on one topic. Uses 'I' in writing. Writes about feelings, judgment or direct experience. Creates characters from experience and immediate environment.

• • • • • • • • • • • • • • • • • • • • • • • • • • • • • • • • • • • • • • • • • • • • • • • • • • • • • •

## Writing band D

**What the writer does**

Marks most common words with incorrect spelling when editing writing. Uses ideas, themes and structure from books in writing. Uses concepts of order and time in writing. Reads, rereads and revises own written work. Uses everyday words in appropriate written context.

**What the writing shows**

Punctuation used conventionally. Conventional spelling used most of the time; spelling showing recall of visual patterns. Stories that can be read, understood and retold by classmates. Several sentences constructed on one topic in a logical order. A smooth connection of ideas. Beginning, middle and end in narrative writing.

**Use of writing**

Writes stories containing characters from outside personal environment. Writes with ease on most matters of personal experience. Writes on a variety of topics. Writes personal anecdotes and letters to friends. Writes for a known audience. Uses a range of written forms — poems, letters, journals, logs, etc.

• • • • • • • • • • • • • • • • • • • • • • • • • • • • • • • • • • • • • • • • • • • • • • • • • • • • • •

## Writing band E

**What the writer does**

Edits work to a point where others can read it; corrects common spelling errors, punctuation and grammatical errors. Develops ideas into paragraphs. Uses a dictionary, thesaurus or word-checker to extend and check vocabulary for writing. Uses vivid, specific language.

**What the writing shows**

Sentences with ideas that flow. Paragraphs with a cohesive structure. Ability to present relationships and to argue or persuade. Messages in expository and argumentative writing identifiable by others, although some information may be omitted. Brief passages written with clear meaning, accuracy of spelling and apt punctuation. Appropriate shifts from first to third person in writing. Consistent use of the correct tense. Appropriate vocabulary for familiar audiences such as peers, younger children or adults, with only occasional inappropriate word choice. Compound sentences, using conjunctions. Variations of letters, print styles or fonts. A print style appropriate to task and consistent handwriting style.

**Use of writing**

Writes a properly sequenced text that has a convincing setting. Creates characters from imagination.

## Matthew

Matthew's writing samples are illustrated beside the teacher's profile ratings.

| WRITING | | | | | | | | |
|---|---|---|---|---|---|---|---|---|
| **PROFILE BAND RATINGS** | | | | | | | | |
| **A** | **B** | **C** | **D** | **E** | **F** | **G** | **H** | **I** |
| ⓪ | ⓪ | ⓪ | ⓪ | ⓪ | ● | ● | ● | ● |
| ① | ① | ① | ① | ● | ① | ① | ① | ① |
| ② | ② | ● | ● | ② | ② | ② | ② | ② |
| ● | ● | ③ | ③ | ③ | ③ | ③ | ③ | ③ |

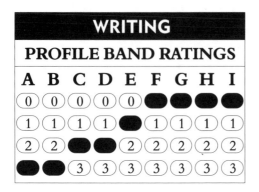

*Octpben 12, 1992*

*I got sk oh the bs.*

*Matt*

*Matt*
*I luv rogr rabit*
*it is fune I*
*lac the Purt vin*
*he ses a nus*
*woo min*

Matthew is a nine-year-old boy who is labelled 'learning disabled' in order to receive special education services. He attended special class in the 1992–93 school year and came to the class in September 1993 knowing most sounds, but unable to blend sounds together to read. He loved to be read to and had a great fascination with books. By June 1994 he was reading using context clues, self-correcting and interacting tremendously with his selected books.

His writing grew just as solidly. His teacher feels that Matthew will be able to return to the regular classroom in another year or two, as he gains in confidence and skill. The teacher used a highlighter pen also to illustrate his progress in both reading and writing; these records were shown to his parents, together with the writing samples. The writing records (with the highlighted sections shaded in the profile record) are shown below.

What the teacher is illustrating in these assessments of Darren and Matthew is that the profiles allow the students' progress and growth to be monitored regardless of the issues of normative comparisons.

# Writing Profile Rocket

Class ..................................... School .............................

Teacher ................................... Student ......... *Matthew*

**I** • • • • • • Writes in many genres. Masters the craft of writing. Is capable of powerful writing.

Is aware of subtleties in language. Develops analytical arguments. Uses precise description in writing. Edits to sharpen meaning. • • • • • • **H**

**G** • • • • • • Uses rich vocabulary, and writing style depends on topic, purpose and audience. Writing is also lively and colorful. Can do major revisions of writing.

Can describe things well. Can skillfully write and tell a story or describe phenomena. Now has skills to improve writing. • • • • • • **F**

**E** • • • • • • Can plan, organize and polish writing. Writes in paragraphs. Voaculary and grammar are suited to topic. Can write convincing stories.

Can write own stories. Changes words and spelling until satisfied with the result. • • • • • • **D**

**C** • • • • • • Now says something in own writing. Is writing own sentences. Is taking interest in appearence of writing.

Is learning about handwriting. Knows what letters and words are and can talk about ideas in own writing. Is starting to write recognizable letters and words. • • • • • • **B**

**A** • • • • • • Knows that writing says something. Is curious about environmental print. Is starting to see patterns.

50% of the Grade ☐ students can be located within this range. Norms for all grades can be identified by locating the 'box' from the box and whisker plot in Chapter 13 for the relevant skill.

The student is estimated to be at about this location on the profile. See the worked example for writing shown on pages 106-8.

*Figure 11.2*

Profiles emphasise the positive; they allow the teacher and the parents to focus on what a student is achieving, not on the failures.

Darren and Matthew are in a self-contained classroom; many other identified students spend at least part of their school day in the mainstream classroom. For the teachers of special students, close communication between the classroom teacher and special education staff is critical.

# Writing Profile Record

Class ................................................. School ...........................................
Name ............... *Matthew* ................ Term .............................................

## Writing band C

### What the writer does

Commences writing without assistance. Has a personalized handwriting style that meets most handwriting needs. Checks written work by reading it aloud. Sounds out words as an aid to spelling.

### What the writing shows

Legible writing with recognizable words. Words put together in sentence format. Words written in a logical order to make a sentence that can be read. Upper- and lower-case letters used conventionally. Written sentences that can be understood by an adult.

### Use of writing

Sentences convey message on one topic. Uses 'I' in writing. Writes about feelings, judgment or direct experience. Creates characters from experience and immediate environment.

- - - - - - - - - - - - - - - - - - - - - - - - - - - - - - - - - - - - - - - - - - - - - - - - -

## Writing band D

COMMENT

### What the writer does

Marks most common words with incorrect spelling when editing writing. Uses ideas, themes and structure from books in writing. Uses concepts of order and time in writing. Reads, rereads and revises own written work. Uses everyday words in appropriate written context.

### What the writing shows

Punctuation used conventionally. Conventional spelling used most of the time; spelling showing recall of visual patterns. Stories that can be read, understood and retold by classmates. Several sentences constructed on one topic in a logical order. A smooth connection of ideas. Beginning, middle and end in narrative writing.

### Use of writing

Writes stories containing characters from outside personal environment. Writes with ease on most matters of personal experience. Writes on a variety of topics. Writes personal anecdotes and letters to friends. Writes for a known audience. Uses a range of written forms — poems, letters, journals, logs, etc.

- - - - - - - - - - - - - - - - - - - - - - - - - - - - - - - - - - - - - - - - - - - - - - - - -

## Writing band E

COMMENT

### What the writer does

Edits work to a point where others can read it; corrects common spelling errors, punctuation and grammatical errors. Develops ideas into paragraphs. Uses a dictionary, thesaurus or word-checker to extend and check vocabulary for writing. Uses vivid, specific language.

### What the writing shows

Sentences with ideas that flow. Paragraphs with a cohesive structure. Ability to present relationships and to argue or persuade. Messages in expository and argumentative writing identifiable by others, although some information may be omitted. Brief passages written with clear meaning, accuracy of spelling and apt punctuation. Appropriate shifts from first to third person in writing. Consistent use of the correct tense. Appropriate vocabulary for familiar audiences such as peers, younger children or adults, with only occasional inappropriate word choice. Compound sentences, using conjunctions. Variations of letters, print styles or fonts. A print style appropriate to task and consistent handwriting style.

### Use of writing

Writes a properly sequenced text that has a convincing setting. Creates characters from imagination.

# CHAPTER 12
# The reading classroom

## Assessment as a natural part of teaching and learning

Classrooms are busy places where in the course of daily activities — the culture of the classroom, the interactions of the learners with others in the classroom, the production of oral and written texts, the teacher's and children's understanding of the learning process, and the classroom setting itself — all have a part to play. The reading classroom described in this section — a Grade 5–6 classroom described in some detail — is no exception; however, the structure and information-gathering processes could be typical of other grade levels, and this will be demonstrated.

In this group, students chose books from the class library, the school library and their personal libraries both for silent reading time and for reading at home because of the teacher's belief that the opportunity to read self-selected materials silently should occur every day. Silent reading, demonstrated by role models such as the teacher, the principal and parents, was vital to show the students that reading was valued. The actual daily timetabling of silent reading reinforced its importance and provided time for reading that might not otherwise have happened in busy lives. The students kept reading logs, which provided evidence of the numbers and kinds of books read. These texts were discussed in groups, and sometimes with the teacher. The teacher also chose books to read to the students: books that enabled them to develop strategies — or ways of thinking about texts — in order to see them as meaningful and to take pleasure in how and what their reading made them think.

The students were readers who had already learned how to use the semantic, syntactic and graphophonic cueing systems described in a sociopsycholinguistic approach to reading. The school was very supportive of the profile approach to assessment and had adopted it in its school policy. The teachers liked the fact that the profile scale was developed to enable them to focus on achievements and outcomes in learning in a way that allowed for the idiosyncrasies of individual students as they developed their reading skills.

The literacy profiles had been chosen because the school administration realized that their use would overcome some of the difficulties inherent — as they saw the situation — in reading tests and comprehension tests per se. There were seen to be important differences between reading as it occurs in tests and reading as it occurs in everyday life. Reading-test passages are usually much shorter than those in everyday texts, and the cognitive processing used to integrate a shorter text is different and less elaborate than that used in a longer one. Also, a good reader is someone who can resist the emotional appeals of a text by understanding how it works. Reading passages used in tests tend to be matter of fact, emotionally neutral, and able to be handled objectively. The literacy profiles allowed for the collection of data about the students' reading when the teaching and learning was taking place. The indicators of development accumulated in an observable fashion as the students' reading abilities progressively emerged and their knowledge of the reading process expanded.

## John: a pen picture

The following example shows, in more detail, how the teacher used the literacy scale to synthesize information from broad descriptions of the reading and learning behavior of a ten-year-old student, John. Initially the teacher began to form a picture of John's reading strategies and habits from work samples, reading lists and end-of-year descriptive reports from his previous teacher and his parents. This information would be very unwieldy but for the indicators on the scale, which provide a manageable way of rating progress. The indicators are evidently present in the student's work and they provide a common vocabulary for describing progress.

John had come into the class with a report that described him as 'not very interested and unwilling to work consistently'. (Unhelpful descriptions like this were quite usual reading before the profiles provided common criteria for teachers to focus on in discussion). He liked reading information books in silent reading time, but had a history of being distracted and of annoying others when he was

# Reading band C

### Reading strategies
Rereads a paragraph or sentence to establish meaning. Uses context as a basis for predicting meaning of unfamiliar words. Reads aloud, showing understanding of purpose of punctuation marks. Uses picture cues to make appropriate responses for unknown words. Uses pictures to help read a text. Finds where another reader is up to in a reading passage.

### Responses
Writing and artwork reflect understanding of text. Retells, discusses and expresses opinions on literature, and reads further. Recalls events and characters spontaneously from text.

### Interest and attitudes
Seeks recommendations for books to read. Chooses more than one type of book. Chooses to read when given free choice. Concentrates on reading for lengthy periods.

# Reading band D

### Reading strategies
Reads material with a wide variety of styles and topics. Selects books to fulfil own purposes. States main idea in a passage. Substitutes words with similar meanings when reading aloud. Self-corrects, using knowledge of language structure and sound–symbol relationships. Predicts, using knowledge of language structure and/or sound/symbol to make sense of a word or phrase.

### Responses
Discusses different types of reading materials. Discusses materials read at home. Tells a variety of audiences about a book. Uses vocabulary and sentence structure from reading materials in written work as well as in conversation. Uses themes from reading in artwork. Follows written instructions.

### Interest and attitudes
Recommends books to others. Reads often. Reads silently for extended periods.

supposed to be listening to a story. His handwriting was poorly formed, without a personal style. In his self-evaluation at the beginning of the year he wrote, 'I listen good and I talk good but when I read I sometimes get stuck on the words'. He indicated that he wasn't keen on writing because he had difficulty spelling words conventionally.

John was placed on the profile's reading scale at the beginning of the school year. The teacher used a highlighter pen to show these attributes; here the highlighted sections are indicated with shading. This highlighting of what the student can do is more powerful than a checklist, which seems to emphasise what the student has yet to learn.

Although John represents the students at the lower end of the scale in this class, he does have basic reading strategies.

John's profile shows that he has established most of the behaviors described in reading band C. He is able to use all the strategies needed as a reader to seek meaning. In fact, he is showing many strategies indicated in reading band D. He is able to identify the main idea in a passage and select books to fulfil his own purposes, although these purposes do not include reading fiction for pleasure. The profiles are formative here because

they show that it is in the areas of response and attitude that there are gaps in John's reading behavior, and this points to ways in which he could be helped. He needs to learn the pleasures of reading fiction: to be turned on to story. There are some problems with self-esteem, which probably have resulted from concentration by a previous teacher on surface features such as spelling and handwriting. These demand attention.

That the profiles place assessment in a teaching and learning context is shown in the case of John by the fact that the teacher is the assessment instrument who collects information throughout the school day. The assessment program has a wash-back effect on the teaching and learning contexts: the students need to encounter literature and respond to it, so the first context is whole-class discussion of literature sessions, when the teacher reads aloud serials or shorter picture-story books and initiates discussion. Such sessions are used often as times to help students find appropriate ways to think about and discuss their reading. The adult or more expert peer would support the cognitive work of the child, focusing his or her attention on the main points, scaffolding towards solution. In these large-group experiences the

# Reading Profile Rocket

Class ............................................. School ..............................................

Teacher ........................................... Student ...... *John* ...........................

Is skillful in analyzing and interpreting own response to reading. Can respond to a wide range of text styles.

Is clear about own purpose for reading. Reads beyond literal text and seeks deeper meaning. Can relate social implications to text.

Reads for learning as well as pleasure. Reads widely and draws ideas and issues together. Is developing a critical approach to analysis of ideas and writing.

Is familiar with a range of genres. Can interpret, analyze and explain responses to text passages.

Will tackle difficult texts. Writing and general knowledge reflects reading. Literary response reflects confidence in settings and characters.

Expects and anticipates sense and meaning in text. Discussion reflects grasp of whole meanings. Now absorbs ideas and language.

Looks for meaning in text. Reading and discussion of text shows enjoyment of reading. Shares experience with others.

Recognizes many familiar words. Attempts new words. Will retell story from a book. Is starting to become an active reader. Interested in own writing.

Knows how a book works. Likes to look at books and listen to stories. Likes to talk about stories.

I H G F E D C B A

50% of the Grade ☐ students can be located within this range. Norms for all grades can be identified by locating the 'box' from the box and whisker plot in Chapter 13 for the relevant skill.

The student is estimated to be at about this location on the profile. See the worked example for writing shown on pages 106-8.

*Figure 12.1*

teacher demonstrates strategies that helped understanding of the process. John needs to learn the pleasures of reading, which include predicting, finding clues, interpreting signs and arguing about the author's intent; these are some of the ways in which readers construct texts. He needs to take risks and understand that reading starts with individual response, which is pleasurable, to refine through social construction of meaning in a group. He needs to find out that his contributions to group discussions will be valued and used in a joint construction of meaning.

Further questions broaden the picture of John's beliefs and reinforce the view that his strategic knowledge is sound.

| When you come to something you do not know, what do you do? | *When I come to something I have problems with, I sometimes read the sentence again and figure out what the word is.* |
| If you knew someone was having difficulty, how would you help that person? | *I'd ask them to sound the word out and keep trying. But if they can't, I'd tell them.* |

This questioning allows the teacher to find out about the students' views of what it is to be a reader. The teacher believes that there is a complex relationship between student's knowledge and thinking, and teaching: the students' conceptions about reading — its nature, purposes and functions — are a result of interaction between their prior knowledge about reading and the reading events experienced in the classroom.

## Elizabeth

A reading inventory was used to collect more data to help determine the 'starting point' of understanding. Each student in the class was surveyed concerning his or her beliefs about or attitudes to reading; for example, they were asked to indicate the particular reasons they thought someone was a good reader, and what they themselves could do to improve as readers. The following extract is from Elizabeth's written interview at the start of the year.

| What makes her a good reader? | *She is a good reader because she speaks loudly and holds her book lower than her face.* |
| What would you like to do better as a reader? | *I could speak louder and lower my book.* |

These answers indicate Elizabeth's concern with oral reading behavior; because everyone had concentrated on getting her to raise her normally quiet voice, this aspect of reading had come to assume undue importance. She had become even more reluctant to participate in discussions.

## Jason

Teachers of beginning readers should learn the attributes in the early bands and keep the first nutshell statements in mind as they help their students to become readers. Jason's teacher kept some anecdotal records of his first months at school and placed them in a portfolio for future reference.

*October 16*    *Jason still resists coming together with the group for storytime. He is very active and restless. He hasn't been read to at home and his mother reports that he isn't interested in reading his take-home books with her. I have had a talk to him about being good to his mother and reading her a story.*

*October 18*    *When we were all reading the big book The Hungry Giant, Jason started taking an interest when they were reading loudly, 'I'll hit you with my bommy-knocker'. He began to join in, too.*

*October 20*    *Jason and Chuck had two copies of Mem Fox's Possum Magic and were checking to see if Hush was missing in the same picture in each book. They borrowed a copy each of Margaret Mahy's The Lion in the Meadow. Who wants to match rabbit's ears as a pre-reading activity. You have to learn how books work.*

*November 2*    *Jason and Jane were sorting and arranging the Dr. Seuss books. They browsed through some and discussed the jokes, helped by the pictures. He is now one of the first to come for storytime and sits entranced. The power of story!*

*December 10*    *Jason's mother told me today that he never misses 'reading' with her now. She reads the book to him first. When he reads to me he is starting to talk about the letters in his name that are the starting ones for words in the book. He also recognizes a few words e.g the, see, fish, too. He has been reading the books made in class in silent reading time and talking about them. I wrote in his Log book that he could be encouraged to point as he was reading to get the idea of one to one.*

## Reading band A

### Concepts about print
Holds book the right way up. Turns pages from front to back. On request, indicates the beginnings and ends of sentences. Distinguishes between upper- and lower-case letters. Indicates the start and end of a book.

### Reading strategies
Locates words, lines, spaces, letters. Refers to letters by name. Locates own name and other familiar words in a short text. Identifies known, familiar words in other contexts.

### Responses
Responds to literature (smiles, claps, listens intently). Joins in familiar stories.

### Interests and attitudes
Shows preference for particular books. Chooses books as a free-time activity.

## Reading band B

COMMENT

### Reading strategies
Takes risks when reading. 'Reads' books with simple, repetitive language patterns. 'Reads', understands and explains own 'writing'. Is aware that print tells a story. Uses pictures for clues to meaning of text. Asks others for help with meaning and pronunciation of words. Consistently reads familar words and interprets symbols within a text. Predicts words. Matches known clusters of letters to clusters in unknown words. Locates own name and other familiar words in a short text. Uses knowledge of words in the environment when 'reading' and 'writing'. Uses various strategies to follow a line of print. Copies classroom print, labels, signs, etc.

### Responses
Selects own books to 'read'. Describes connections among events in texts. Writes, role-plays and/or draws in response to a story or other form of writing (e.g. poem, message). Creates ending when text is left unfinished. Recounts parts of text in writing, drama or artwork. Retells, using language expressions from reading sources. Retells with approximate sequence.

### Interests and attitudes
Explores a variety of books. Begins to show an interest in specific type of literature. Plays at reading books.

---

The teacher highlighted Jason's reading profile.

## Tanya

Tanya is in Grade 2. She had had many book experiences before starting school and learned to read very easily. This year seems to have been one of consolidation for Tanya; there are only a few new attributes on her reading profile. She has continued to be an avid reader and her log shows that she is reading denser and longer texts. There is evidence that she likes to reread books read by the teacher to the class.

The following comments are taken from transcriptions of discussions after being read stories by Anthony Browne.

*April 15* Commenting on Anthony Browne's *Willy the Wimp*: 'The ending was a big surprise. I thought he had got really strong. He's a hero and then bang. But he had been a hero in a way'.

*April 18* Commenting on Anthony Browne's *Gorilla*: 'I'm catching on to Anthony Browne. People can be like animals. She

### Tanya's reading log

| Date | Title and author | Parent's comment | Teacher's comment |
|------|------------------|------------------|-------------------|
| April 5 | *Peace at Last* by Jill Murphy | Enjoyed the humor. | Read to group. |
| April 16 | *Possum Magic* by Mem Fox | Talked about illustrations. | Read to group. |
| April 17 | *Oliver Button is a Sissy* by Tomie de Paola | Said, 'This is the longest book I've read'. | Read her first chapter book. |

*wanted her father to be nice like the gorilla and when she got up there's a banana in his pocket to show it. In Piggybook the pigs are the father and the boys when they are bad'.* Tanya has demonstrated that familiarity with an author's works enables her to make connections that help her interpret meaning, but she hasn't yet the experience to explain these very clearly. Her enjoyment is enhanced through close looks at texts. Tanya's profile would show progress as far as band B in her responses to reading, but her strategies include those found in band D.

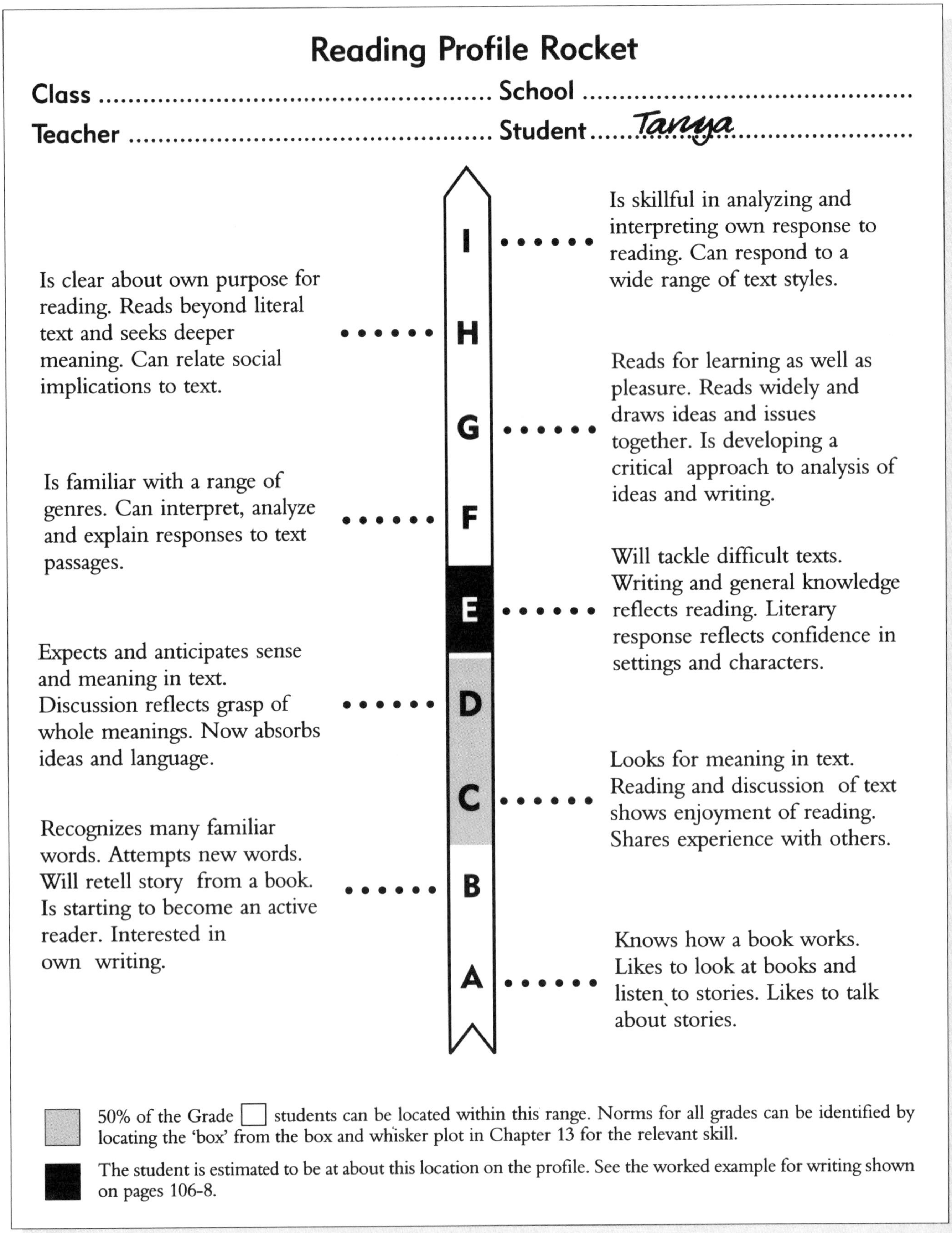

# Reading Profile Rocket

Class ................................................ School ................................................

Teacher ............................................ Student ...... *Tanya* ..........................

**I** ・・・・・・ Is skillful in analyzing and interpreting own response to reading. Can respond to a wide range of text styles.

Is clear about own purpose for reading. Reads beyond literal text and seeks deeper meaning. Can relate social implications to text. ・・・・・・ **H**

**G** ・・・・・・ Reads for learning as well as pleasure. Reads widely and draws ideas and issues together. Is developing a critical approach to analysis of ideas and writing.

Is familiar with a range of genres. Can interpret, analyze and explain responses to text passages. ・・・・・・ **F**

**E** ・・・・・・ Will tackle difficult texts. Writing and general knowledge reflects reading. Literary response reflects confidence in settings and characters.

Expects and anticipates sense and meaning in text. Discussion reflects grasp of whole meanings. Now absorbs ideas and language. ・・・・・・ **D**

**C** ・・・・・・ Looks for meaning in text. Reading and discussion of text shows enjoyment of reading. Shares experience with others.

Recognizes many familiar words. Attempts new words. Will retell story from a book. Is starting to become an active reader. Interested in own writing. ・・・・・・ **B**

**A** ・・・・・・ Knows how a book works. Likes to look at books and listen to stories. Likes to talk about stories.

☐ 50% of the Grade ☐ students can be located within this range. Norms for all grades can be identified by locating the 'box' from the box and whisker plot in Chapter 13 for the relevant skill.

■ The student is estimated to be at about this location on the profile. See the worked example for writing shown on pages 106-8.

*Figure 12.2*

# The class group

The profiles help teaching and reporting in a way that is consistent with good teaching practise because they enhance the quality of communication in regard to achievement, attitudes, skills, strategies used and so on. These things are not easily described by any test scores, but the progress of Jason, Elizabeth, Tanya and John is easily documented from a wealth of evidence. The profiles crystallize and record the information gained by the teacher as test-instrument.

Essentially, student profiles are built by teachers simply teaching and observing the students in the classroom. No further changes need to be made to the daily routine. Teachers teach. They ask questions, set work to be done, give tests, collect work from the students, conference with the students. All the time they are gathering information about the students. Sometimes they are not even aware that they are collecting assessment information. Irregular reference to profile statements helps them to interpret information collected routinely as part of the teaching process. Sometimes the teacher needs to take time to note direct observations; the notes can include details of who is being observed and the context of observation. The following extract is part of a teacher's notes on the class.

> The group were very excited and had difficulty practicing polite turn-taking in the small-group discussion. Amber barely waited for the previous speaker to finish as her thoughts raced along. Kirsten, normally very patient, joined in excitedly. They all listened with the usual respect to Max, but most unusually, John and Amber challenged his view, once again rushing to speak. They didn't convince him but they are becoming really confident that their interpretation can be just as right as Max's.

Other notes were references to circumstances or events that provided useful information. These included moods, health and personal events.

> Amber told me today that they had to talk the music teacher into making a better time for concert practise. 'The other grades didn't care but we didn't want to miss Literature Groups'. It's probably fortunate that John is the music teacher's son! She is very excited about his change in attitude to reading this year.

As the volume of observation grows, it is possible for the teacher to see patterns emerging in the reading processes — sometimes individual patterns, sometimes group patterns. To briefly summarize, in the two short extracts quoted above it is possible to discover indicators of quality talk, attitude to reading, the social structure of the classroom and engagement in explaining and defending of understanding. The teacher can now refer to the profiles for pointers of group response to reading and other reading behavior that is evident when group work is used as a class activity.

The central focus is on the students as thinkers, exploring and helping each other move beyond initial understandings and their personal responses to new interpretations and broadening of world views in transactions with specific texts. Sometimes audiotapes were made of the discussions. This is well illustrated in the following extract.

| | |
|---|---|
| **Elizabeth** | *The ending was funny. I suppose it meant he had to be an emu to have another big bird for a mate.* |
| **John** | *He hadn't seen an emu before so he didn't know it was the best thing to be.* |
| **Max** | *It was about the best thing to be is yourself. Be satisfied. The illustrator really made Edward look like a lion and a snake but I felt sad and embarrassed for him. It wasn't going to work, all that copying.* |
| **John** | *The snake was best.* |
| **Kirsten** | *I was thinking all the time about why doesn't some kid in the crowd call out that there's an ostrich in the monkey cage or the reptile house. That would be what would happen for real.* |
| **Max** | *In real life if you pretend you're clever or something, no one says anything. They're too polite.* |
| **Kirsten** | *I suppose the author is saying that even if you are great at pretending and it seems natural, it's still better to be yourself and things will turn out better.* |
| **Elizabeth** | *And meet another emu.* |

This text showed Elizabeth taking on her usual role of initiating the discussion by introducing her puzzlement about the ending of the picture storybook and John suggesting a solution. He is joining in quite naturally now. Max continues to build on their connections, and used his own feelings to discuss the protagonist's lack of success in finding his real self. Kirsten has listened and considered an anomaly — and why the author/illustrator has made this decision — and Max picks up on her line of thought. Elizabeth makes a small joke — unusual for her. They have discussed the meaning of life as readers making transactions with text. They have become readers who have considered philosophical issues about perception as they make transactions with text.

Even the brief, previous discussion of the students' responses implies that the teacher is bringing legitimate, tacit knowledge to the interpretation of the situation. Because the teacher is a human instrument, she is able to bring this experiential knowledge of the students into use. John's predictions near the end of the book show him shaping his final predictions, although some wish fulfillment is still apparent rather than deep transactions with the text.

*I think Trotter will come and get Gilly or Gilly's mum will come and see Gilly. Gilly might run away from her grandmother's house. Trotter and W.E. and Mr Randolph might come and live with Gilly and her grandmother.*

Given information from only a small cross-section of John's reading activities, it is easy to see his progress. He now knows the excitement of tackling a difficult text. He is beginning to have confidence in predicting and talking about the setting, point of view and other ways in which the text influences the reader. He is starting to explain his responses. His teacher has by now been able to highlight all the indicators in bands C and D, and he is showing many in band E and some in band F.

All students keep what are called journals. These are portfolios of work that include some reflective writing. In an effort to get away from the view of response as 'doing an interesting activity at the end', different strategies are tried.

Students were introduced to the idea of think-alouds (illustrated below) as a way to show what questioning and image-making was going on in their heads as they read. These think-alouds have several advantages over other types of verbal reporting; they lessen the problem of memory failure, since the reporting is nearly concurrent with the process being described, and they are highly specific to the task and so produce reliable results. The students were asked to try these think-alouds on several occasions, but they found them tedious and so were not asked to use the technique very often. John's think-aloud gives evidence of active transactions that show how much he has now learned about the process.

*I can see him in a striped prisoner suit. What an exaggeration. He's going on a bit much about being sent to a cattery. I'm into it here. The author must really be showing us what an exaggerator he is. I'm still wondering what his revenge will be. Perhaps he'll go on holiday without them. No. That's stupid. He is a cat. It'll have to be something a real cat would do normally and it will look like he's done it on purpose.*

On occasions, the students were asked to write 'before' and 'after' predictions for the text. They were also asked to write their responses after a chapter had been read. These personal responses were often used in group discussion to help in the social construction of new meaning and final understanding of the text.

The following example illustrates how these kinds of data become available. Amber's response after reading shows her using personal feelings to interpret the puzzles and the metaphor of the seeds, and then come to an understanding of life cycles.

*I can understand why Sam doesn't want to go back to the Red Rocks because if I had been looking after my sister and had gone away for a minute and when I got back and found she was gone, I wouldn't want to go back there. The only reason why Mum, Dad and Grandpa could go and see the marble carving by the rocks was because they didn't want Sam to think it was his fault. Life goes on even if your loved ones die. Sometimes you have just to forget about the past and concentrate on the future. The seeds that Sam blows away are a sort of sign that life goes on and new life starts.*

# Writing Profile Class Record

Class .................. 5 .......... School .. Krystal Heights ...............................

Teacher ............... Ms Hammond ...........................................

| Band | | John | Stephanie | Daniel | Kirsten | Elizabeth | Angus | Amber | Max | | | | | | | | | | | | | |
|---|---|---|---|---|---|---|---|---|---|---|---|---|---|---|---|---|---|---|---|---|---|
| **I** | Writes in many genres. Masters the craft of writing. Is capable of powerful writing. | | | | | | | | | | | | | | | | | | | | |
| **H** | Is aware of subtleties in language. Develops analytical arguments. Uses precise description in writing. Edits to sharpen meaning. | | | | | | | | | | | | | | | | | | | | |
| **G** | Uses rich vocabulary, and writing style depends on topic, purpose and audience. Writing is also lively and colorful. Can do major revisions of writing. | | | | | | | | | | | | | | | | | | | | |
| **F** | Can describe things well. Can skillfully write and tell a story or describe phenomena. Now has skills to improve writing. | | | | | | | | | | | | | | | | | | | | |
| **E** | Can plan, organize and polish writing. Writes in paragraphs. Vocabulary and grammar are suited to topic. Can write convincing stories. | | | | | | | | | ▮ | ▮ | | | | | | | | | | |
| **D** | Can write own stories. Changes words and spelling until satisfied with the result. | | | ▮ | | ▮ | ▮ | ▮ | | | | | | | | | | | | | |
| **C** | Now says something in own writing. Is writing own sentences. Is taking interest in appearance of writing. | | ▮ | | ▮ | | | | | | | | | | | | | | | | |
| **B** | Is learning about handwriting. Knows what letters and words are and can talk about ideas in own writing. Is starting to write recognizable letters and words. | | | | | | | | | | | | | | | | | | | | |
| **A** | Knows that writing says something. Is curious about environmental print. Is starting to see patterns. | | | | | | | | | | | | | | | | | | | | |

*Figure 12.3*

# CHAPTER 13
# Establishing normative data on teacher judgment

Monitoring learning can occur at a number of levels in an education system, and for several purposes. Within the classroom, we can monitor performance levels of individuals to ensure that they are making progress and that their levels of performance are within the expected standard for their year or age group.

At the building level, it is possible for buildings to obtain evidence regarding overall standards and trends in performance over time. For example, building reporting in terms of profiles to districts, states or national systems can be provided with data from participating schools in a form that enables them to compare their achievement levels with state or district norms.

The ways in which profiles are used for monitoring purposes should be governed by the consequences for those involved. Where the stakes are low, local school building-focused assessment linked to the profiles is likely to be a highly cost-effective means of obtaining comparable information on standards, and could be the way in which buildings generally respond to the challenge of monitoring standards and evaluating programs.

Where the stakes are high, however, as in system-level monitoring of standards, some will argue that it may be inappropriate to rely entirely upon classroom-based teacher judgments. But this argument also applies to any system that relies on a single approach to assessment in high-stakes exercises. It is just as inappropriate to rely on one test in any area of learning — no matter how many items it contains, the test is a one-time assessment; specially developed tests or assessment tasks that facilitate reporting in terms of the profiles are needed so that a consistent approach is developed. Then there is the so called 'objective' test measure, and the wide-ranging assessment based on continuous observation and professional judgment. The standardized objective test can be used as another form of moderation: this is statistical moderation. Because of the research that has shown that the reliability of teacher judgement grows over time, it is possible to advise systems that monitor educational standards to take the opportunity to modify their survey testing programs and use reporting in terms of the profiles as well as in terms of their own tests. Similar results can be expected — higher and higher reliabilities of teacher judgments.

Teachers from many schools in many states have assisted us in providing ratings for the profiles. The ratings illustrate the students' progress in language arts, using the profiles as a basis. The method of collecting the data was relatively simple; the instructions that were given to teachers are presented below.

---

Read the description of reading-related behavior in the profile bands labelled A through I. Compare each student's behavior pattern with the patterns described at each band level and use the following codes.

3   If the student has established the behavior pattern and consistently exhibits all or most of the behavior in the band, use code 3.

2   If the student is developing behavior patterns such that some but not all of the behavior for a band is often exhibited, use a code of 2 for that band.

1   If the student is beginning to show some of the behaviour pattern of a band level in that only a little of the pattern is shown, use a code of 1 for that band.

0   If the student shows none of the behavior patterns for a band level, use a code of 0 for that band.

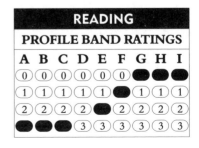

# Writing Profile Class Record

Class ......... 4 ......... School *Krystal Heights* ...........

Teacher ......... *Ms Hammond* ...........

Students: John, Stephanie, Daniel, Kirsten, Elizabeth, Angus, Amber, Max

| Band | Description |
|---|---|
| **I** | Is skillful in analyzing and interpreting own response to reading. Can respond to a wide range of text styles. |
| **H** | Is clear about own purpose for reading. Reads beyond literal text and seeks deeper meaning. Can relate social implications to text. |
| **G** | Reads for learning as well as pleasure. Reads widely and draws ideas and issues together. Is developing a critical approach to analysis of ideas and writing. |
| **F** | Is familiar with a range of genres. Can interpret, analyze and explain responses to text passages. |
| **E** | Will tackle difficult texts. Writing and general knowledge reflect reading. Literacy response reflects confidence in settings and characters. |
| **D** | Expects and anticipates sense and meaning in text. Discussion reflects grasp of whole meanings. Now absorbs ideas and language. |
| **C** | Looks for meaning in text. Reading and discussion of text shows enjoyment of reading. Shares experience with others. |
| **B** | Recognizes many familiar words. Attempts new words. Will retell story from a book. Is starting to become an active reader. Interested in own writing. |
| **A** | Knows how a book works. Likes to look at books. and listen to stories. Likes to talk about stories. |

*Figure 13.1*

The following table shows the ratings for a small group from a Grade 6 class at the start of the school year. All students were rated 3 (established) in bands A and B and all were rated 0 (no evidence) in band G, so these extremes are not presented.

**Rating patterns of students in a small group**

|  | Band C | Band D | Band E | Band F |
|---|---|---|---|---|
| John | 2 | 1 | 0 | 0 |
| Stephanie | 3 | 2 | 0 | 0 |
| Daniel | 2 | 2 | 1 | 0 |
| Kirsten | 3 | 2 | 1 | 0 |
| Elizabeth | 3 | 2 | 1 | 0 |
| Angus | 3 | 2 | 1 | 0 |
| Amber | 3 | 2 | 1 | 1 |
| Max | 3 | 2 | 2 | 1 |

The teacher could quickly place Max, an example of a very keen ten-year-old reader, on the reading scale. Max has been described in all his previous reports as a quietly confident leader in both small and large groups. He has many interests, being a keen sportsman and a talented musician who sings in the choir and plays the piano, the guitar and the saxophone. He has many experiences to bring to his reading. Max writes in his self-evaluation that he particularly enjoys writer's workshop times and wants to be a writer like his father. His mother is a keen reader and they often talk about books together. His reading log showed her influence in encouraging him to read classics such as *Treasure Island*, although he makes interesting choices of his own. Max has established all reading behaviors indicated in band C, is developing those in bands D and E and is beginning to use some of the strategies listed in band F. These indicators synthesize much of the information that can be gained intuitively from the above description. Max is shown to be a reader who can talk about what he has read. He absorbs language and ideas. He knows how to tackle a difficult text and read silently for extended periods. Figure 13.1 shows how these ratings are mapped onto the profiles for an overview of a class. Adjustments can be made when teachers judge that progress is evident: the adjustment is simply a matter of adding to the felt-pen mark on the profile. The advantages of passing this class-level information from teacher to teacher are many.

This has further applications when ratings are collected from many schools; a series of box and whisker plots can be used to present the data and to establish norms. A box and whisker plot provides a simple way of presenting normative data and distributions of scores on the profile scales.

Using the rating scale for the profiles in this way enables plots of the data to be produced representing patterns across schools or districts. The box and whisker plots present several pieces of information (Figure 13.2). For each group, the 10th and 90th percentiles are drawn at the end of the 'whiskers'. The box marks off the 25th and 75th percentiles and the median is marked by a point inside the box. As such, the plots present several distributions simultaneously and allow comparisons across year levels. The star indicates the median score of the distribution.

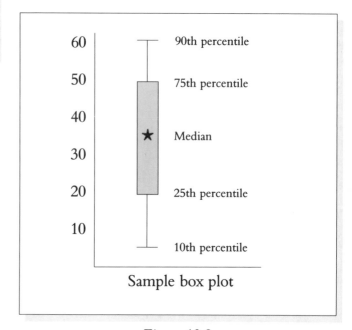

*Figure 13.2*

A series of schools were surveyed and ratings were gathered from teachers over a large range of classes. Box and whisker plots for reading, writing and spoken language scales are presented in Figure 13.3. Approximately 1000 students were rated in twenty-seven schools across the United States and larger numbers of students have been surveyed in Ireland and Australia; however although these should not be considered norms in the true sense of the word, the similarity in the distributions and box plots is striking.

Information of the type represented in Figure 13.3 gives a picture of the progress of *groups of students*. The graphs indicate a period of rapid growth over the first few years of schooling, coinciding with the period during which young people acquire basic literacy skills. Thereafter, a steady and consistent rate of growth is indicated up to Year 10. It is noticeable, however, that the range of achievement increases markedly over the

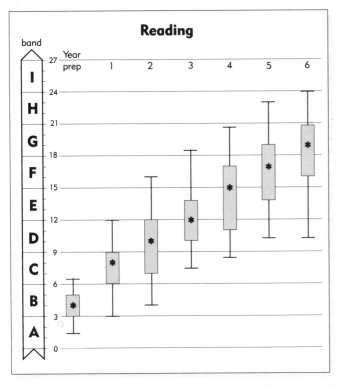

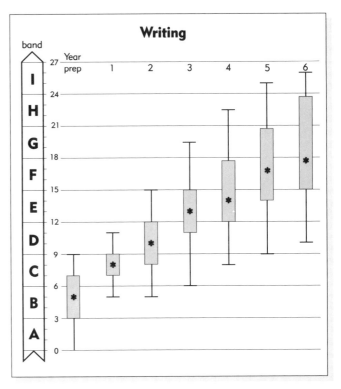

Figure 13.3   Literacy achievement levels

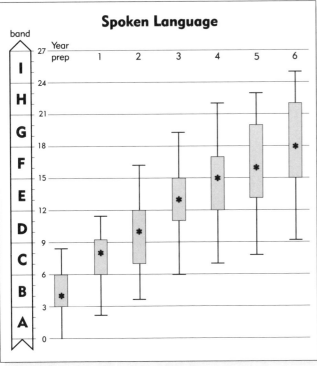

early years of schooling, with more than four levels separating students at the 10th and 90th percentiles. A feature of the graph is the flat growth trajectory for low-achieving students. It shows that achievement levels of students at the 10th percentile increase by less than one band between Years 4 to 10. These charts have been used to establish the normative regions in the rockets, the class records and the growth charts used in Chapter 10.

Given the cumulative nature of the scales, the established behaviors should reflect this. Students can be developing more than one band-level behaviour at any one time; reading development is a continuous process, and the time of the school year needs to be stipulated. If these figures represented the whole system it is evident that by the spring, when most data were collected, the number of students in the system that had fully developed each band level and progressed towards literacy could be stipulated. This would have some implications for curriculum planning and could be treated in much the same way as a cumulative score distribution on a standardized test. Of more interest, however, is the proportion of students who are still developing behaviors or skills at each band level. This can be interpreted as the instructional level of the students.

# APPENDIX 1
# Nutshell statements for profiles

| Band | Reading | Writing | Spoken language | Listening | Viewing |
|---|---|---|---|---|---|
| **A** | Knows how a book works. Likes to look at books and listen to stories. Likes to talk about stories. | Knows that writing says something. Is curious about environmental print. Is starting to see patterns. | Understands social conventions of spoken language. Initiates and responds appropriately. | Listens attentively, interacts with the speaker and responds with interest. | Recalls events from visual texts with familiar content. |
| **B** | Recognizes many familiar words. Attempts new words. Will retell story from a book. Is starting to become an active reader. Interested in own writing. | Is learning about handwriting. Knows what letters and words are and can talk about ideas in own writing. Is starting to write recognizable letters and words. | Experiments and uses language in a variety of ways. Uses talk to clarify ideas and experiences. Body language assists in conveying understanding. | Listens for a range of purposes, discriminates sounds in words and can recall stories told. | Enjoys retelling meaning from visual texts with predictive narrative structure. Has favorite characters. |
| **C** | Looks for meaning in text. Reading and discussion of text shows enjoyment of reading. Shares experience with others. | Now says something in own writing. Is writing own sentences. Is taking interest in appearance of writing. | Is developing confidence with spoken language. Is sensitive to voice control in specific situations. | Is developing confidence through active listening, responding and clarifying when meaning is not clear. | Uses various strategies to interpret visual texts. Enjoys talking about events and characters. |
| **D** | Expects and anticipates sense and meaning in text. Discussion reflects grasp of whole meanings. Now absorbs ideas and language. | Can write own stories. Changes words and spelling until satisfied with the result. | Can recount and retell, recite with feeling and use a range of vocabulary to arouse and maintain audience interest. | Distinguishes between social and informational listening; will seek clarification. | Discusses and interprets relationships between ideas, information and events in visual texts designed for special viewing. |
| **E** | Will tackle difficult texts. Writing and general knowledge reflect reading. Literary response reflects confidence in settings and characters. | Can plan, organize and polish writing. Writes in paragraphs. Vocabulary and grammar are suited to topic. Can write convincing stories. | Uses logic, argument and questioning to clarify ideas and understanding appropriate to audience and purpose. | Accepts others' opinions and is developing listening strategies — listening for relationships in stories, poems, etc. | Selects and uses strategies, appropriate for making meaning, that are appropriate for different texts and viewing purposes. |

| Band | Reading | Writing | Spoken language | Listening | Viewing |
|------|---------|---------|-----------------|-----------|---------|
| **F** | Is familiar with a range of genres. Can interpret, analyze and explain responses to text passages. | Can describe things well. Can skillfully write and tell a story or describe phenomena. Now has skills to improve writing. | Can persuade and influence peers, using language. Clarifies and orders thoughts. Shows expression of ideas, feelings, opinions, and ability to generalize or hypothesize. Speech contains inferences from varied situations. | Links stories and spoken forms of language to values. Is aware of relevance and irrelevance, pitch, intensity, and intonation. | Discusses themes and issues in visual texts, allowing for varying interpretations. Discusses possible reasons for this. |
| **G** | Reads for learning as well as pleasure. Reads widely and draws ideas and issues together. Is developing a critical approach to analysis of ideas and writing. | Uses rich vocabulary, and writing style depends on topic, purpose, and audience. Writing is lively and colorful. Can do major revisions of writing. | Uses language increasingly to explore ideas, question and summarize discussions. Uses tone to create effect and to aid communication. | Explores and reflects on ideas while listening; is becoming familiar with a range of spoken forms of language and is able to distinguish between them for purpose, meaning, and appropriate audience. | Explores different perspectives on complex issues through viewing a range of texts. Considers the contexts in which texts were constructed, and how the texts reflect them. |
| **H** | Is clear about own purpose for reading. Reads beyond literal text and seeks deeper meaning. Can relate social implications to text. | Is aware of subtleties in language. Develops analytical arguments. Uses precise description in writing. Edits to sharpen meaning. | Uses and appreciates nuances of language to affect an audience. Monitors and modifies communication to aid understanding. | Distinguishes emotive rhetoric from reasoned argument. Spoken genres are analyzed for meaning and underlying messages. | Considers a variety of interrelationships between texts, contexts, viewers, and makers of visual texts. Constructs meaning from a range of visual texts and justifies this with detailed and well-chosen evidence from the texts. |
| **I** | Is skillful in analyzing and interpreting own response to reading. Can respond to a wide range of text styles. | Writes in many genres. Masters the craft of writing. Is capable of powerful writing. | Uses language proficiently in its many forms. Is able to evaluate and respond to content and points of view. | Is a skilled listener, able to distinguish emotive and persuasive rhetoric and to analyze a wide range of spoken genres while listening. | Analyzes and criticizes visual texts for a range of purposes and audiences. |

| Band | Reading | Writing | Spoken language |
|------|---------|---------|-----------------|
| **A** | **Concepts about print**<br>Holds book the right way up. Turns pages from front to back. On request, indicates the beginnings and ends of sentences. Distinguishes between upper- and lower-case letters. Indicates the start and end of a book.<br><br>**Reading strategies**<br>Locates words, lines, spaces, letters. Refers to letters by name. Locates own name and other familiar words in a short text. Identifies known, familiar words in other contexts.<br><br>**Responses**<br>Responds to literature (smiles, claps, listens intently). Joins in familiar stories.<br><br>**Interests and attitudes**<br>Shows preference for particular books. Chooses books as a free-time activity. | **What the writer does**<br>Uses writing implement to make marks on paper. Explains the meaning of marks (word, sentence, writing, letter). Copies 'words' from signs in immediate environment. 'Reads', understands and explains own 'writing'.<br><br>**What the writing shows**<br>Understanding of the difference between picture and print. Use of some recognizable symbols in writing.<br><br>**Use of writing**<br>Comments on signs and other symbols in immediate environment. Uses a mixture of drawings and 'writing' to convey and support an idea. | **Uses of language**<br>Listens attentively to stories, songs and poems. Reacts to stories, songs and poems heard in class (smiles and comments). Joins in familiar songs, poems and chants. Allows others to speak without unnecessary interruption. Waits for appropriate turn to speak. Offers personal opinion in discussion. Speaks fluently to the class. Follows instructions, directions and explanations.<br><br>**Features of language**<br>Connects phrases and clauses with 'and', 'and then', 'but'. Speaks at a rate that enables others to follow. Speaks at a volume appropriate to the situation. |
| **B** | **Reading strategies**<br>Takes risks when reading. 'Reads' books with simple, repetitive language patterns. 'Reads', understands and explains own 'writing'. Is aware that print tells a story. Uses pictures for clues to meaning of text. Asks others for help with meaning and pronunciation of words. Consistently reads familar words and interprets symbols within a text. Predicts words. Matches known clusters of letters to clusters in unknown words. Locates own name and other familiar words in a short text. Uses knowledge of words in the environment when 'reading' and 'writing'. Uses various strategies to follow a line of print. Copies classroom print, labels, signs, etc.<br><br>**Responses**<br>Selects own books to 'read'. Describes connections among events in texts. Writes, role-plays and/or draws in response to a story or other form of writing (e.g. poem, message). Creates ending when text is left unfinished. Recounts parts of text in writing, drama or artwork. Retells, using language expressions from reading sources. Retells with approximate sequence.<br><br>**Interests and attitudes**<br>Explores a variety of books. Begins to show an interest in specific type of literature. Plays at reading books. Talks about favorite books. | **What the writer does**<br>Reproduces words from signs and other sources in immediate environment. Holds pencil/pen using satisfactory grip. Uses preferred hand consistently for writing. Attempts to put 'words' in 'sentence' format. 'Writes' a simple message. Uses sound–symbol linkages. 'Captions' or 'labels' drawings.<br><br>**What the writing shows**<br>Use of vocabulary of print (letters, words, question marks, etc.). Use of letters of the alphabet and other conventional symbols. Use of letters in groups to form words. Placing of spaces between groups of 'letters'. Knowledge that writing moves from left to right in lines from top to bottom of page.<br><br>**Use of writing**<br>Writes own name.<br><br>**Interests and attitudes**<br>Understands that writing is talk written down. | **Uses of language**<br>Makes short announcements clearly. Tells personal anecdotes in discussion. Retells a story heard in class, preserving the sequence of events. Accurately conveys a verbal message to another person. Responds with facial expressions. Responds with talk when others initiate conversation. Initiates conversation with peers. Holds conversation with familiar adults. Asks what unfamiliar words mean. Uses talk to clarify ideas or experience.<br><br>**Features of language**<br>Reacts to absurd word-substitution. Demonstrates an appreciation of wit. Reacts to unusual features of language such as rhythm, alliteration or onomatopoeia. |
| **C** | **Reading strategies**<br>Rereads a paragraph or sentence to establish meaning. Uses context as a basis for predicting meaning of unfamiliar words. Reads aloud, showing understanding of purpose of punctuation marks. Uses picture cues to make appropriate responses for unknown words. Uses pictures to help read a text. Finds where another reader is up to in a reading passage. | **What the writer does**<br>Commences writing without assistance. Has a personalized handwriting style that meets most handwriting needs. Checks written work by reading it aloud. Sounds out words as an aid to spelling. | **Uses of language**<br>Makes verbal commentary during play or other activities with concrete objects. Speaks confidently in formal situations (assembly, report to class). Explains ideas clearly in discussion. Discusses information heard (e.g. dialogue, news items, report). Based on consideration of what has already been said, offers personal opinions. Asks for repetition, restatement or general explanation to clarify meaning. |

| Band | Reading | Writing | Spoken language |
|------|---------|---------|-----------------|

**C**
(cont.)

### Reading

**Responses**

Writing and artwork reflect understanding of text. Retells, discusses and expresses opinions on literature, and reads further. Recalls events and characters spontaneously from text.

**Interests and attitudes**

Seeks recommendations for books to read. Chooses more than one type of book. Chooses to read when given free choice. Concentrates on reading for lengthy periods.

### Writing

**What the writing shows**

Legible writing with recognizable words. Words put together in sentence format. Words written in a logical order to make a sentence that can be read. Upper- and lower-case letters used conventionally. Written sentences that can be understood by an adult.

**Use of writing**

Sentences convey message on one topic. Uses 'I' in writing. Writes about feelings, judgment or direct experience. Creates characters from experience and immediate environment.

### Spoken language

**Features of language**

Sequences a presentation in logical order. Gives instructions in a concise and understandable manner. Reads aloud with expression, showing awareness of rhythm and tone. Modulates voice for effect. Nods, looks at speaker when others initiate talk.

---

**D**

### Reading

**Reading strategies**

Reads material with a wide variety of styles and topics. Selects books to fulfil own purposes. States main idea in a passage. Substitutes words with similar meanings when reading aloud. Self-corrects, using knowledge of language structure and sound–symbol relationships. Predicts, using knowledge of language structure and/or sound/symbol to make sense of a word or a phrase.

**Responses**

Discusses different types of reading materials. Discusses materials read at home. Tells a variety of audiences about a book. Uses vocabulary and sentence structure from reading materials in written work as well as in conversation. Uses themes from reading in artwork. Follows written instructions.

**Interests and attitudes**

Recommends books to others. Reads often. Reads silently for extended periods.

### Writing

**What the writer does**

Marks most common words with incorrect spelling when editing writing. Uses ideas, themes and structure from books in writing. Uses concepts of order and time in writing. Reads, rereads and revises own written work. Uses everyday words in appropriate written context.

**What the writing shows**

Punctuation used conventionally. Conventional spelling used most of the time; spelling showing recall of visual patterns. Stories that can be read, understood and retold by classmates. Several sentences constructed on one topic in a logical order. A smooth connection of ideas. Beginning, middle and end in narrative writing.

**Use of writing**

Writes stories containing characters from outside personal environment. Writes with ease on most matters of personal experience. Writes on a variety of topics. Writes personal anecdotes and letters to friends. Writes for a known audience. Uses a range of written forms — poems, letters, journals, logs, etc.

### Spoken language

**Uses of language**

Tells personal anecdotes, illustrating in a relevant way the issue being discussed. Recounts a story or repeats a song spontaneously. Retells scenes from a film or drama. Offers predictions about what will come next. Recites poems. Asks questions in conversation. Has a second try at something to make it more precise. Arouses and maintains an audience interest during formal presentations (e.g. report to class, announcement).

**Features of language**

Uses a range of vocabulary related to a particular topic. Maintains receptive body stance in conversation. Speaks in a way that conveys feelings (while keeping emotions under control).

---

**E**

### Reading

**Reading strategies**

Reads to others with few inappropriate pauses. Interprets new words by reference to suffixes, prefixes and meaning of word parts. Uses directories such as a table of contents or an index, or telephone and street directories, to locate information. Uses library classification systems to find specific reading materials.

**Responses**

Improvises in role play, drawing on a range of text. Writing shows meaning inferred from the text. Explains a piece of literature. Expresses and supports an opinion on whether an author's point of view is valid. Discusses implied motives of characters in the text. Makes comments and expresses feelings about characters. Rewrites information from text in own words. Uses text as a model for own writing. Uses a range of books and print materials as information sources for written work. Reads aloud with expression.

### Writing

**What the writer does**

Edits work to a point where others can read it; corrects common spelling errors, punctuation and grammatical errors. Develops ideas into paragraphs. Uses a dictionary, thesaurus or word-checker to extend and check vocabulary for writing. Uses vivid, specific language.

**What the writing shows**

Sentences with ideas that flow. Paragraphs with a cohesive structure. Ability to present relationships and to argue or persuade. Messages in expository and argumentative writing identifiable by others, although some information may be omitted. Brief passages written with clear meaning, accuracy of spelling and apt punctuation. Appropriate shifts from first to third person in writing. Consistent use of the correct tense. Appropriate vocabulary for familiar audiences such as peers, younger children or adults, with only occasional inapp-ropriate word choice. Compound sentences, using conjunctions. Variations of letters, print styles or fonts. A print style appropriate to task and a consistent handwriting style.

**Use of writing**

Writes a properly sequenced text that has a convincing setting. Creates characters from imagination.

### Spoken language

**Uses of language**

Presents a point of view to a large audience. Presents materials with consideration for audience needs. Speculates and puts forward a tentative proposition. Uses logic, arguments or appeals to feelings to persuade others. Explores concepts related to concrete materials by describing, narrating or explaining how things work and why things happen. Dramatizes familiar stories, showing understanding. Uses convincing dialogue to role-play short scenes involving familiar situations or emotions. Invites others to participate. Takes initiative in raising new aspects of an issue. Asks questions to elicit more from an individual. Answers questions confidently and clearly in interviews. Asks for the meaning of familiar words used in unfamiliar ways.

**Features of language**

Makes links between ideas in discussions. Uses complex connectives in speech, such as 'although', 'in spite of', 'so that'. Uses syntactical structures — principal and subordinate clauses. Uses vocabulary appropriate to audience and purpose. Distinguishes between words of similar meaning.

---

| Band | Reading | Writing | Spoken language |
|------|---------|---------|-----------------|

## F

### Reading strategies

Describes links between personal experience and arguments and ideas in text. Selects relevant passages or phrases to answer questions without necessarily reading whole text. Formulates research topics and questions and finds relevant information from reading materials. Maps out plots and character developments in novels and other literary texts. Varies reading strategies according to purposes for reading and nature of text. Makes connections between texts, recognising similarities of themes and values.

### Responses

Discusses author's intent for the reader. Discusses styles used by different authors. Describes settings in literature. Forms generalizations about a range of genres, including myth, short story. Offers reasons for the feelings provoked by a text. Writing and discussions acknowledge a range of interpretations of text. Offers critical opinion or analysis of reading passages in discussion. Justifies own appraisal of a text. Synthesizes and expands on information from a range of texts in written work.

### What the writer does

Writes sentences in different forms: statement, question, command, explanation. Writes paragraphs to develop logical sequence of ideas. Corrects most spelling, punctuation and grammatical errors in editing others' written work. Consults available sources to improve or enhance writing. Joins letters, using linkages where appropriate, to form personal hand-writing style.

### What the writing shows

Narratives containing introduction, complication and resolution in a logical order. Longer descriptions and narratives developed coherently. Use of both active and passive voice. A range of vocabulary and grammatical structures. Complex sentences — principal and subordinate clauses. Higher level writing skills in areas of special interest. Understanding of the difference between narrative and other forms of writing.

### Use of writing

Completes standard forms requiring personal information. Makes appropriate use of narrative and other forms of writing.

### Uses of language

Asks speaker to clarify ambiguities. Asks questions about words of similar meanings. Elicits information or reaction or opinions from others in conversation. Asks questions to draw information from the group. Indicates disagreement in a constructive manner. Attempts to resolve disagreement or misunderstanding. Supports constructively the statements of others. Attempts to keep discussion on the topic. Makes formal introductions with courtesy and clarity. Tells a story with expression and emphasis, showing confidence, highlighting key points and demonstrating the storyteller's art. Explores abstract ideas (justice, good and evil) by generalizing, hypothesizing or inferring.

### Features of language

Uses a range of idiomatic expressions with confidence. Reacts to an inappropriate choice of words. Makes positive interjections.

## G

### Reading strategies

Reads manuals and literature of varying complexity. Interprets simple maps, tables and graphs in the context of discursive text. Makes generalizations and draws conclusions from reading. Reads at different speeds, using scanning, skim-reading or careful reading as appropriate.

### Responses

Supports argument or opinion by reference to evidence presented in sources outside text. Compares information from different sources. Identifies opposing points of view and main and supporting arguments in text. Comments on cohesiveness of text as a whole. Discusses and writes about author's bias and technique. In writing, offers critical opinion or analysis of reading materials. Distils and links ideas from complex sentences and paragraphs.

### Interests and attitudes

Reads widely for pleasure, for interest or for learning.

### What the writer does

Writes in narrative, expository and argumentative styles. Uses a range of writing styles effectively and appropriately for purpose, situation and audience. Uses a range of vocabulary effectively and appropriately for purpose, situation and audience. Edits work to improve the smooth flow of ideas and reorganizes work to make it more readable. Replaces words and sentences during revision of written work. Changes sequence of ideas, adds new ideas during revision.

### What the writing shows

Main and supporting ideas presented clearly. Correct format for letters, invitations. Figurative language, such as simile, for descriptive purposes.

### Use of writing

Shows a range of styles — written conversations, poems, plays, journals. Writes formal and social letters and distinguishes between the purposes of each. Adapts writing to demands of task. Completes complex forms that seek detailed biographical and related information.

### Uses of language

Asks interview questions that are relevant. Extends another group member's contribution by elaboration or illustration. Helps others to put forward ideas. Summarizes the conclusions reached in a group discussion. Takes initiative in moving discussion to the next stage. Reflects and evaluates discussion (e.g. What have we learnt? How did we do it?). Asks speakers for background information. Dramatizes scenes from complex stories, showing understanding of dramatic structure. Role-plays/improvizes shaped scenes, showing understanding of dramatic structure. Talks or writes about moral of story heard.

### Features of language

Uses new words spontaneously. Varies tone, pitch, pace of speech to create effect and aid communication. Self-corrects to remove the effects upon audience of a poor choice of words. Comments on some ways in which spoken language differs from written language (e.g. repetitions, colloquialisms, slang, emphasis, incomplete utterances). Talks or writes about special forms of language, such as accents or dialects.

## H

### Reading strategies

Compiles own list of needed references, using bibliographies and literature-search techniques. Interprets material at different levels of meaning. Forms generalizations about a range of genres, including myth, short story. Lists a wide variety of sources read for specific learning tasks.

### Responses

Identifies plot and subplot. Identifies allegory. Formulates hypothetical questions about a subject, based on prior reading. Compares and offers critical analysis of materials presented in the media. Extracts ideas embedded in complex passages of text. Displays critical opinion and analysis in written reports of

### What the writer does

Edits and revises own work to enhance effect of vocabulary, text organization and layout. Edits and revises others' writing, improving presentation and structure without losing meaning or message.

### What the writing shows

Meaning expressed precisely. Organization and layout of written text accurate and appropriate for purpose, situation and audience. Argument, description and narrative presented effectively and appropriately. Vocabulary showing awareness of ambiguities and shades of meaning. Figurative language, such as metaphor, to convey meaning.

### Uses of language

Experiments with and reflects on possible readings and interpretations of a piece of scripted drama. Sustains cogent arguments in formal presentation. Holds conversation with less familiar adults (e.g. guest speaker).

### Features of language

Attempts special forms of language, such as accents or dialects, in own written dialogue. Defines or explains words to cater for audience needs. Comments on bias or point of view in spoken language. Analyzes factors that contribute to the success or otherwise of discussion.

| Band | Reading | Writing | Spoken language |
|------|---------|---------|-----------------|

**H**
(cont.)

reading. Identifies different authors' points of view on a topic. Reformulates a task in the light of available reading resources. Questions and reflects on issues encountered in texts. Shows understanding by being able to adopt an alternative point of view to the author's. Discusses styles used by different authors.

**I**

### Reading strategies

Examines situational meaning of text. Explores a range of meaning dependent on the combination of influences of writer, reader and situation.

### Responses

Explains textual innuendo and undertone. Interprets analogy, allegory and parable in text. Identifies and explains deeper significance in text. Defends each interpretation of text. Discusses and writes about author's bias. Analyzes cohesiveness of text as a whole.

### What the writer does

Writes with ease on most familiar topics in both short passages and extended writing. Uses analogies and symbolism in writing. Uses irony in writing. Uses figures of speech, metaphor and simile to illustrate and support message embedded in extended text. Structures a convincing argument in writing. Can use sustained and elaborated metaphorical language in writing.

### What the writing shows

Extension beyond conventions of standard written English in a skillful and effective way.

### Use of writing

Conveys extended arguments through writing. Adapts to demands of academic writing.

### Uses of language

Makes effective use of visual or other materials to illustrate ideas. Capitalizes on opportunities offered by responses to interview questions. Asks interview questions designed to elicit extended responses.

### Features of language

Talks or writes about subtle effects of dialogue between characters in film or drama. Uses puns and double meanings. Comments on tone, attitude or emphasis in speech. Talks about quality of speech, such as loudness, pitch, pronunciation, articulation and dialect.

| Band | Listening | Viewing |
|---|---|---|

## A

### How the listener attends
Attends to oral stories, poems, etc.

### What the listener does
Recognizes sounds in the environment. Begins to recall detail. Begins to sequence. Follows directions during classroom routines, such as clean-up.

### What the listener demonstrates
Hearing sounds and doing actions simultaneously in action songs. Hearing rhyming words. Using thinking skills in listening activities to sense emotion, predict and sequence.

### Viewing strategies
Focuses on illustration (for details). Recognizes TV program introduction. Tells own story from well-known picture book. Retells own story from favorite TV program.

### Responses
Joins in to accompany speech/song of favorite TV characters. Joins in to accompany speech/song of favorite story characters. Values illustrations as enjoyment. Values television as enjoyment.

### Interests and attitudes
Enjoys a variety of illustrations. Has particular television interests.

## B

### How the listener attends
Listens for a variety of purposes. Listens and sustains attention for increasing periods. Focuses on whole (context) rather than part (detail) when listening to a story.

### What the listener does
Hears initial and final sounds of words.

### What the listener demonstrates
Recall of information from stories, poems, films, etc. Mental pictures while listening to stories, poems, etc. Identification of meaning through speaker's voice (anger, surprise). Thinking skills in listening activities, selecting and giving opinions.

### Concepts
Is beginning to realize that parts can make a whole

### Strategies
Predicts from visuals; predicts during television program. Is beginning to pay attention to important details. Is beginning to read rebus. Recognizes environmental signs in context.

### Responses
Is beginning to respond to visual information. Is beginning to talk about characters in illustrations. Is beginning to talk about characters on tape.

### Interests
Enjoys talking about favorite illustrations. Enjoys learning about favorite cartoons. Enjoys talking about favorite TV programs. Enjoys computer games.

## C

### How the listener attends
Listens to others. Begins to show interest in what people have to say. Is aware of non-verbal communication. Is learning to listen critically for main idea and supporting details.

### What the listener does
Hears middle sounds in words.

### What the listener demonstrates
Awareness of the need to be silent, to wait and respond as appropriate. Ability to distinguish between types of speech (a chat, a warning, a joke). Thinking skills in listening activities to plan, compare and begin to make judgments.

### Concepts
Uses visuals to follow directions. Is beginning to realize information can be gained.

### Strategies
Uses rebus. Is beginning to project into others' experience.

### Responses
Is beginning to interpret main idea.

### Interests
Recognizes work of a favorite illustrator. Recognizes types of cartoons. Relates why enjoys particular television programs. Is beginning to enjoy Logo.

## D

### How the listener attends
Hears the difference between social interactions and information transaction.

### What the listener does
Hears consonants, vowels, blends and digraphs. Hears the difference between hard and soft vowels.

### What the listener demonstrates
Awareness of facts, details, feelings, and values. Ability to listen to and recognize and give an explanation (e.g. in science). Need for repetition or an explanation when meaning is unclear. Thinking skills in listening activities to make judgments, summarize and evaluate.

### Concepts about visuals
Is beginning to recognize that not everything on screen is true. Knows there is a message in advertisement.

### Strategies
Uses webs to aid comprehension. Uses webs to access prior knowledge. Develops coded messages.

### Responses
Describes TV character(s) vividly. Can interpret main idea. Can describe main idea.

### Interests and attitudes
Has a rationale for favorite TV programs. Is expanding knowledge about cartoons. Is developing recognition of illustrator styles.

## E

### How the listener attends
Is interested in someone else's point of view. Develops strategies for listening to instructions (mental pictures, step by step, etc.). Begins to listen to another person's opinion — to listen for what is important.

### What the listener does
Identifies the sounds of vowels, consonants, digraphs and blends. Uses awareness of sounds to identify consonants, vowels. Uses sounds to identify prefixes, suffices, compounds and syllables.

### Concepts about visuals
Is beginning to make references with a variety of visual representations.

### Strategies
Can focus on details but keep whole in mind. Classifies TV programs viewed. States reasons for selecting TV program. Uses a rating scale (school/home devised) and explains why a rating was given. Has rationale for favorite illustrators and artists. Names many forms of visual representation.

| Band | Listening | Viewing |
|------|-----------|---------|

## E
(cont.)

### What the listener demonstrates

Listening skills to compare and find relationships in stories, poems and conversations. Thinking skills in listening activities, to analyze and hypothesize.

### Responses

Relates to people's real contribution. Identifies the 'message' in commercials.

### Interests and attitudes

Is beginning to understand viewer discrimination. Enjoys describing personal opinion of an illustrator's work. Is developing ability to classify video games.

## F

### How the listener attends

Uses values when listening to a story or explanation (animal activities/hunter). Listens for difference between relevance and irrelevance. Listens to pros and cons of argument.

### What the listener does

Distinguishes intensity, pitch, quality and sequence of a variety of sounds.

### What the listener demonstrates

Thinking skills in listening activities, to hypothesize.

### Concepts about visuals

Recognizes the difference between TV fact and fiction. Is beginning to understand function of various visual forms.

### Strategies

Is beginning to understand purposes for different program categories. Is beginning to hypothesize about meaning of visual representation. Applies many forms of visual representation.

### Responses

Is beginning to relate own opinion to those of a critic. Is realizing and identifying a variety of forms of advertisements.

### Interests and attitudes

Relates reasons for viewer discrimination. Continues to view and discuss work of a number of illustrators.

## G

Not yet developed.

Recognizes scenes that shape the viewer's understanding of a character's role (e.g. identifies scenes that establish a character as a leader). Makes generalizations about the complexities of a character's personality from behavior. Retells a pivotal event and explains its significance to the narrative.

## H

Not yet developed.

Understands the interaction between actors' real lives and their constructed film roles (e.g. speculates on the reason for an actor not appearing in a sequel). Empathizes with two characters by inferring from visual clues the nature and context of their relationship (e.g. constructs a dialogue between two characters in a poster). Infers and evaluates the narrative connection between two pieces of viewed text.

## I

Not yet developed.

Understands that authors are sensitive to social concerns when constructing written and reviewed texts (e.g. understands why a girl was added to the book and an Aboriginal girl to the film sequel). Integrates information from related written and viewed sources (e.g. uses information from the film and text extract to explain an inference that a character draws). Interprets and evaluates an image using information from another viewed source (e.g. judges the relationship between a film and a poster of a sequel to the film). Detects and describes complex feelings in a viewed text (e.g. recognizes a character's emotional ambivalence).

# Blackline masters

# Reading Profile Rocket

Class ......................................... School ..........................................

Teacher ...................................... Student ........................................

**I** ...... Is skillful in analyzing and interpreting own response to reading. Can respond to a wide range of text styles.

Is clear about own purpose for reading. Reads beyond literal text and seeks deeper meaning. Can relate social implications to text. ...... **H**

**G** ...... Reads for learning as well as pleasure. Reads widely and draws ideas and issues together. Is developing a critical approach to analysis of ideas and writing.

Is familiar with a range of genres. Can interpret, analyze and explain responses to text passages. ...... **F**

**E** ...... Will tackle difficult texts. Writing and general knowledge reflect reading. Literary response reflects confidence in settings and characters.

Expects and anticipates sense and meaning in text. Discussion reflects grasp of whole meanings. Now absorbs ideas and language. ...... **D**

**C** ...... Looks for meaning in text. Reading and discussion of text shows enjoyment of reading. Shares experience with others.

Recognizes many familiar words. Attempts new words. Will retell story from a book. Is starting to become an active reader. Interested in own writing. ...... **B**

**A** ...... Knows how a book works. Likes to look at books and listen to stories. Likes to talk about stories.

50% of the Grade [ ] students can be located within this range. Norms for all grades can be identified by locating the 'box' from the box and whisker plot in Chapter 13 for the relevant skill.

■ The student is estimated to be at about this location on the profile. See the worked example for writing shown on pages 106-8.

# Writing Profile Rocket

Class ................................................. School .............................................

Teacher .............................................. Student............................................

**I** • • • • • • Writes in many genres. Masters the craft of writing. Is capable of powerful writing.

Is aware of subtleties in language. Develops analytical arguments. Uses precise description in writing. Edits to sharpen meaning. • • • • • • **H**

**G** • • • • • • Uses rich vocabulary, and writing style depends on topic, purpose and audience. Writing is lively and colorful. Can do major revisions of writing.

Can describe things well. Can skillfully write and tell a story or describe phenomena. Now has skills to improve writing. • • • • • • **F**

**E** • • • • • • Can plan, organize and polish writing. Writes in paragraphs. Vocabulary and grammar are suited to topic. Can write convincing stories.

Can write own stories. Changes words and spelling until satisfied with the result. • • • • • • **D**

**C** • • • • • • Now says something in own writing. Is writing own sentences. Is taking interest in appearance of writing.

Is learning about handwriting. Knows what letters and words are and can talk about ideas in own writing. Is starting to write recognizable letters and words. • • • • • • **B**

**A** • • • • • • Knows that writing says something. Is curious about environmental print. Is starting to see patterns.

50% of the Grade ☐ students can be located within this range. Norms for all grades can be identified by locating the 'box' from the box and whisker plot in Chapter 13 for the relevant skill.

■ The student is estimated to be at about this location on the profile. See the worked example for writing shown on pages 106–8.

# Spoken Language Profile Rocket

Class ................................................ School ...............................................

Teacher ............................................. Student ..............................................

**I**
Uses language proficiently in its many forms. Is able to evaluate and respond to content and points of view.

Uses and appreciates nuances of language to affect an audience. Monitors and modifies communication to aid understanding.

**H**

**G**
Uses language increasingly to explore ideas, question and summarize discussions. Uses tone to create effect and to aid communication.

Can persuade and influence peers, using language. Clarifies and orders thoughts. Shows expression of ideas, feelings, opinions, and ability to generalize or hypothesize. Speech contains inferences from varied situations.

**F**

**E**
Uses logic, argument and questioning to clarify ideas and understanding appropriate to audience and purpose.

Can recount and retell, recite with feeling and use a range of vocabulary to arouse and maintain audience interest.

**D**

**C**
Is developing confidence with spoken language. Is sensitive to voice control in specific situations.

Experiments and uses language in a variety of ways. Uses talk to clarify ideas and experiences. Body language assists in conveying understanding.

**B**

**A**
Understands social conventions of spoken language. Initiates and responds appropriately.

50% of the Grade ☐ students can be located within this range. Norms for all grades can be identified by locating the 'box' from the box and whisker plot in Chapter 13 for the relevant skill.

■ The student is estimated to be at about this location on the profile. See the worked example for writing shown on pages 106-8.

# Listening Profile Rocket

Class ................................................. School ...............................................

Teacher ............................................. Student...............................................

Is a skilled listener, able to distinguish emotive and persuasive rhetoric and to analyze a wide range of spoken genres while listening.

**I**

Distinguishes emotive rhetoric from reasoned argument. Spoken genres are analyzed for meaning and underlying messages.

**H**

Explores and reflects on ideas while listening; is becoming familiar with a range of spoken forms of language and is able to distinguish between them for purpose, meaning, and appropriate audience.

**G**

Links stories and spoken forms of language to values. Is aware of relevance and irrelevance, pitch, intensity, and intonation.

**F**

Accepts others' opinions and is developing listening strategies — listening for relationships in stories, poems, etc.

**E**

Distinguishes between social and informational listening; will seek clarification.

**D**

Is developing confidence through active listening, responding and clarifying when meaning is not clear.

**C**

Listens for a range of purposes, discriminates sounds in words, and can recall stories told.

**B**

Listens attentively, interacts with the speaker and responds with interest.

**A**

50% of the Grade ☐ students can be located within this range. Norms for all grades can be identified by locating the 'box' from the box and whisker plot in Chapter 13 for the relevant skill.

The student is estimated to be at about this location on the profile. See the worked example for writing shown on pages 106–8.

# Viewing Profile Rocket

Class ..................................................... School ........................................................

Teacher ................................................. Student......................................................

**I** •••••• Analyzes and criticizes visual texts for a range of purposes and audiences.

Considers a variety of interrelationships between texts, contexts, viewers, and makers of visual texts. Constructs meaning from a range of visual texts and justifies this with detailed and well-chosen evidence from the texts. •••••• **H**

**G** •••••• Explores different perspectives on complex issues through viewing a range of texts. Considers the context in which texts were constructed, and how the texts reflect them.

Discusses themes and issues in visual texts, allowing for varying interpretations. Discusses possible reasons for this. •••••• **F**

**E** •••••• Select and use strategies, appropriate for making meaning, that are appropriate for different texts and viewing purposes.

Discusses and interprets relationships between ideas, information and events in visual texts designed for special viewing. •••••• **D**

**C** •••••• Uses various strategies to interpret visual texts. Enjoys talking about events and characters.

Enjoys retelling meaning from visual texts with predictive narrative structure. Has favorite characters. •••••• **B**

**A** •••••• Recalls events from visual texts with familiar content.

50% of the Grade ☐ students can be located within this range. Norms for all grades can be identified by locating the 'box' from the box and whisker plot in Chapter 13 for the relevant skill.

■ The student is estimated to be at about this location on the profile. See the worked example for writing shown on pages 106-8.

# Reading Profile Class Record

Class .......................... School ........................................

Teacher ....................................................................

## Band

| | | |
|---|---|---|
| **I** | Is skillful in analyzing and interpreting own response to reading. Can respond to a wide range of text styles. | |
| **H** | Is clear about own purpose for reading. Reads beyond literal text and seeks deeper meaning. Can relate social implications to text. | |
| **G** | Reads for learning as well as pleasure. Reads widely and draws ideas and issues together. Is developing a critical approach to analysis of ideas and writing. | |
| **F** | Is familiar with a range of genres. Can interpret, analyze and explain responses to text passages. | |
| **E** | Will tackle difficult texts. Writing and general knowledge reflect reading. Literary response reflects confidence in settings and characters. | |
| **D** | Expects and anticipates sense and meaning in text. Discussion reflects grasp of whole meanings. Now absorbs ideas and language. | |
| **C** | Looks for meaning in text. Reading and discussion of text shows enjoyment of reading. Shares experience with others. | |
| **B** | Recognizes many familiar words. Attempts new words. Will retell story from a book. Is starting to become an active reader. Interested in own writing. | |
| **A** | Knows how a book works. Likes to look at books and listen to stories. Likes to talk about stories. | |

# Writing Profile Class Record

Class ........................... School ...................................................
Teacher ........................................................................................

## Band

| Band | Description |
|------|-------------|
| **I** | Writes in many genres. Masters the craft of writing. Is capable of powerful writing. |
| **H** | Is aware of subtleties in language. Develops analytical arguments. Uses precise description in writing. Edits to sharpen meaning. |
| **G** | Uses rich vocabulary, and writing style depends on topic, purpose and audience. Writing is also lively and colorful. Can do major revisions of writing. |
| **F** | Can describe things well. Can skillfully write and tell a story or describe phenomena. Now has skills to improve writing. |
| **E** | Can plan, organize and polish writing. Writes in paragraphs. Vocabulary and grammar are suited to topic. Can write convincing stories. |
| **D** | Can write own stories. Changes words and spelling until satisfied with the result. |
| **C** | Now says something in own writing. Is writing own sentences. Is taking interest in appearance of writing. |
| **B** | Is learning about handwriting. Knows what letters and words are and can talk about ideas in own writing. Is starting to write recognizable letters and words. |
| **A** | Knows that writing says something. Is curious about environmental print. Is starting to see patterns. |

# Spoken Language Profile Class Record

Class ........................... School ............................................................

Teacher ....................................................................................................

## Band

| | | |
|---|---|---|
| **I** | Uses language proficiently in its many forms. Is able to evaluate and respond to content and points of view. | |
| **H** | Uses and appreciates nuances of language to affect an audience. Monitors and modifies communication to aid understanding. | |
| **G** | Uses language increasingly to explore ideas, question and summarize discussions. Uses tone to create effect and to aid communication. | |
| **F** | Can persuade and influence peers, using language. Clarifies and orders thoughts. Shows expression of ideas, feelings, opinions, and ability to generalize or hypothesize. Speech contains inferences from varied situations. | |
| **E** | Uses logic, argument and questioning to clarify ideas and understanding appropriate to audience and purpose. | |
| **D** | Can recount and retell, recite with feeling and use a range of vocabulary to arouse and maintain audience interest. | |
| **C** | Is developing confidence with spoken language. Is sensitive to voice control in specific situations. | |
| **B** | Experiments and uses language in a variety of ways. Uses talk to clarify ideas and experiences. Body language assists in conveying understanding. | |
| **A** | Understands social conventions of spoken language. Initiates and responds appropriately. | |

# Listening Profile Class Record

Class ..................................... School ...................................................................................

Teacher ...............................................................................................................................

## Band

| | | | | | | | | | | | | | | | | | | | | | | |
|---|---|---|---|---|---|---|---|---|---|---|---|---|---|---|---|---|---|---|---|---|---|---|
| **I** Is a skilled listener, able to distinguish emotive and persuasive rhetoric and to analyze a wide range of spoken genres while listening. | | | | | | | | | | | | | | | | | | | | | | |
| **H** Distinguishes emotive rhetoric from reasoned argument. Spoken genres are analyzed for meaning and underlying messages. | | | | | | | | | | | | | | | | | | | | | | |
| **G** Explores and reflects on ideas while listening; is becoming familiar with a range of spoken forms of language and is able to distinguish between them for purpose, meaning, and appropriate audience. | | | | | | | | | | | | | | | | | | | | | | |
| **F** Links stories and spoken forms of language to values. Is aware of relevance and irrelevance, pitch, intensity and intonation. | | | | | | | | | | | | | | | | | | | | | | |
| **E** Accepts others' opinions and is developing listening strategies — listening for relationships in stories, poems, etc. | | | | | | | | | | | | | | | | | | | | | | |
| **D** Distinguishes between social and informational listening; will seek clarification. | | | | | | | | | | | | | | | | | | | | | | |
| **C** Is developing confidence through active listening, responding and clarifying when meaning is not clear. | | | | | | | | | | | | | | | | | | | | | | |
| **B** Listens for a range of purposes, discriminates sounds in words, and can recall stories told. | | | | | | | | | | | | | | | | | | | | | | |
| **A** Listens attentively, interacts with the speaker and responds with interest. | | | | | | | | | | | | | | | | | | | | | | |

# Viewing Profile Class Record

Class ...................... School ..........................................

Teacher ...........................................................................

## Band

| | | |
|---|---|---|
| **I** | Analyzes and criticizes visual texts for a range of purposes and audiences. | |
| **H** | Considers a variety of interrelationships between texts, contexts, viewers, and makers of visual texts. Constructs meaning from a range of visual texts and justifies this with detailed and well-chosen evidence from the texts. | |
| **G** | Explores different perspectives on complex issues through viewing a range of texts. Considers the context in which texts were constructed, and how the texts reflect them. | |
| **F** | Discusses themes and issues in visual texts, allowing for varying interpretations. Discusses possible reasons for this. | |
| **E** | Select and use strategies, appropriate for making meaning, that are appropriate for different texts and viewing purposes. | |
| **D** | Discusses and interprets relationships between ideas, information and events in visual texts designed for special viewing. | |
| **C** | Uses various strategies to interpret visual texts. Enjoys talking about events and characters. | |
| **B** | Enjoys retelling meaning from visual texts with predictive narrative structure. Has favorite characters. | |
| **A** | Recalls events from visual texts with familiar content. | |

# Band continuums

It is important to note that the reading and writing bands do not interrelate; therefore, no comparison should be made between the two.

Student .........................................................................................................

### Reading

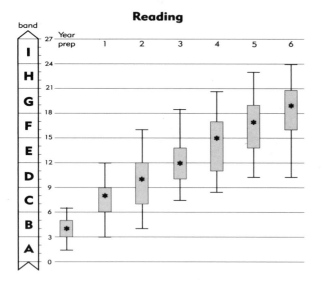

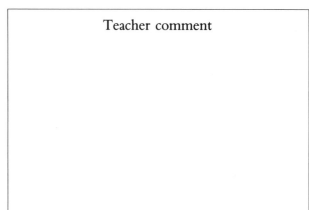

Teacher comment

### Writing

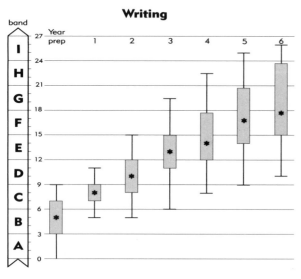

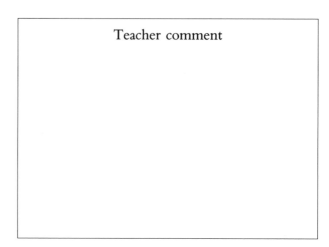

Teacher comment

### Spoken Language

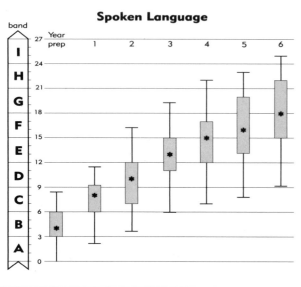

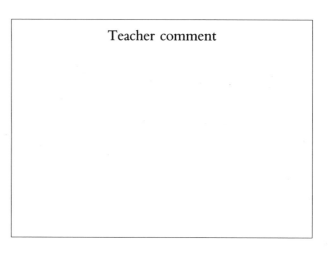

Teacher comment